PRIMARY DESIGN AND TECHNOLOGY
IN PRACTICE

Edited by
Moyra Bentley, Jim Campbell,
Ann Lewis and Mike Sullivan.

Published by Longman Industry and Public Service Management, Longman Group UK Limited, 6th Floor, Westgate House, The High, Harlow, Essex CM20 1YR, England and Associated Companies throughout the world.
Telephone: Harlow (0279) 442601
Fax: Harlow (0279) 444501 Group 3 & 2

British Library Cataloguing in Publication Data
Primary design and technology in practice.
  1. Great Britain. Schools. Curriculum subjects: Science
  2. Great Britain. Schools. Curriculum subjects: Technology
  I. Campbell, James
  507'.1041

  ISBN 0-582-05700-0

  ISBN 0-582-05700-0

Printed and bound in Great Britain by
Biddles Ltd, Guildford and King's Lynn

CONTENTS

Preface

PREFACE

This book comprises a collection of articles on Design and Technology with children from three to eleven. Nearly all have been written by practising teachers, or by lecturers who have been involved in Design and Technology in schools. Ten of the chapters are articles first published (from 1987 onwards) in the journal that we jointly edit, *Education 3-13,* and we have not attempted to alter the original terms (eg, CDT, technology) of the writers. The remaining eight articles were specially written for this book.

Throughout, we have attempted to represent the policy that *Education 3-13* has adopted, of encouraging people to write, clearly and without jargon, about educational practice, in order to raise, and reflect upon, professional issues arising from such practice. We hope that teachers and others facing the challenging task of implementing Design and Technology in the next few years will find the book both helpful and encouraging.

Moyra Bentley, North Riding College
Jim Campbell, University of Warwick
Ann Lewis, University of Warwick
Mike Sullivan, Busill Jones Primary School, Walsall

20 September 1989

PRIMARY DESIGN AND TECHNOLOGY:
an introduction
Moyra Bentley and Jim Campbell

In the field of primary school Design and Technology, we are seeing a re-run of the moral panic about primary science that followed the publication of HMI *Primary Education in England*[1]. This survey had reported that few primary schools were providing a balanced and coherent programme of science for their pupils, despite the existence of innovative and supportive schemes and guides, and substantially funded development projects. The position has improved in respect of science according to the Annual Report for 1987–88 of the Senior Chief Inspector for Schools[2], although it is impossible to tell from the report the extent of improvement. We are told (para. 10) that 'the proportion of schools with scientific work judged to be of a satisfactory or better standard has risen significantly' since 1978, though what the proportion is or what significance is to be attached to 'significantly' remains unclear.

Three major problems

If it has taken a decade to bring about as yet unquantified improvements in primary science, what hope is there for improvement, in Design and Technology, rapid enough to 'deliver' it effectively as one of the foundation subjects of the national curriculum? For on the face of it the current position in respect of Design and Technology is more daunting than that facing Science in 1978 in three ways.

First, primary school teachers knew what was meant by science, and they also knew that the title of the subject, and implicitly its purposes, would not keep changing with every consultation paper. Design and Technology is yet another new name for aspects of what primary teachers have just got used to calling CDT (Craft Design and Technology), and then, following the 1987

Consultation Document[3] on the national curriculum, Technology. There are good reasons for the new name, according to the Interim Report of the Design and Technology Working Group[4]; it represents an attempt to fuse the cognitive and process skills involved in designing and making, craft, and problem solving with a reliance on tools including Information Technology, into one cross-curricular capability - 'the capability to operate creatively in the made world' (para. 1.10). However even this definition understates the contribution of Information Technology, a defect remedied to some extent by the final report of the Working Group which gave a separate profile component to IT.

Second, the problem is not of course only a matter of title and conception; it is also and primarily a disabling sense of their lack of background expertise that affects teachers. In a survey of some 900 teachers concerning their perceived competence to teach the national curriculum subjects[5], Design Technology came lowest, with only 14 per cent feeling competent with their existing level of knowledge. But even this picture gives more grounds for optimism than the harder evidence of 1987 Primary Staffing Survey Tables[6], one of which (Table 9) shows only 700 fulltime primary school teachers, less than 1 per cent of the teaching force, with a qualification in CDT. This is again the lowest percentage in the table, though doubtless some of the teachers qualified in Art/Craft, Science, and Computer Studies would consider themselves competent to contribute to Design and Technology, as conceived of by the Interim Report of the Working Group[4].

A third problem concerns the variable levels of support services to help teachers get started, and to sustain their development in Design and Technology at the primary school level. There is of course some support, but not the level and degree of support from advisers, in-service materials, and guidance that gets through to the majority of classroom teachers, and that helps them gain confidence. At least three kinds of support are needed; training, materials and equipment, and teacher time in school.

The **training** will include the need to extend the knowledge base in the schools, including multi-cultural aspects, assessment and recording skills, and issues associated with equal opportunities. The **materials and equipment** includes simple basic classroom toolkits, more complex equipment especially associated with the control of models, kits, and information technology, and consumables. **Teacher time** will include the need for provision of staff time for in-school development and assessment, together with the deployment of skilled advisory and other support teachers. An example where all these elements have come together within an overall LEA policy commitment is analysed in Chapter Seventeen in this volume. However support at the appropriate level seems uncertain generally, since the equipment needs alone for IT are unlikely to be provided, according to an analysis in the *Times Educational Supplement* (23.6.89), where the attainment targets for IT were shown to be 'undemanding' by comparison with IT demands in English.

Characteristics of primary design and technology

In the mid-1980s, the editors of *Education 3 - 13* commissioned and published a series of articles, (on what we thought of then as CDT) which we hoped would go some way towards helping teachers faced with what was then a need, and is now a requirement, to begin implementing Design and Technology in classrooms. *Education 3 - 13* has, as an objective, encouraging teachers to write reflectively about classroom practice, and the articles we published embodied that objective. They were not merely tips for teachers; they were reports of work teachers had planned and implemented in their classrooms, with the practitioners' reflections on the implications for other teachers wishing to adopt and adapt similar approaches in their own schools. A selection of these articles is included in this volume, together with some specially commissioned material.

The articles incorporate seven characteristics, which amount to an implicit theory of Design and Technology in primary schools. These are:

— that it is mainly a cross-curricular approach to teaching and learning, rather than a subject;
— that it is an investigative, problem-solving activity;
— that it is child-centred in the sense that children's ideas for solutions to problems are starting points to be tested through trying them out;
— that 'imaging'[4] — the representation of ideas as drawings, diagrams, plans, models, prototypes and computer displays and simulations, before their realisation in a product — is a distinctive activity;
— that it is distinctively concerned with knowledge and skills concerning the form and function of materials, artefacts and systems;
— that problems are to be solved in a particular context, environment, or to a particular specification;
— that the activity inevitably involves children in co-operative plannning and communication skills.

We would argue that the above implicit theory has been made explicit in the final report of the Design and Technology working party, which has affirmed the holistic nature of 'Design and Technology Capability'.

For all the above reasons, we think that the requirement to include Design and Technology as a foundation subject in the national curriculum is to be welcomed. For it provides teachers with justification for active learning, for providing children with first hand encounters with real materials, and for starting from children's ideas. We would have preferred to see Design and Technology conceptualised, at least for the first two key stages of the national curriculum, not as a subject, but as a cross-curricular issue. It would have made more sense to think of it that way, for most of those working in primary classrooms. But that has not turned out to be the case, perhaps because there would be problems of status for the subject at secondary level. The analysis provided by Sullivan in Chapter Two in this volume shows how official and semi-official documents, including the Interim and Final reports of the Design and Technology Working Group[4, 7], have tended to emphasise the cross-curricular nature of Design and Technology in primary schools, and that is perhaps enough for our purposes.

There is in addition to the implicit theory of Design and Technology in these articles, an underlying value position about the relationship of human beings to technology and design in society. This is that technology is a way of controlling the environment, not a system by which we are controlled. This position, a fundamental part of the hidden curriculum of primary technology, is always implicit in the articles in this volume, and often quite explicit.

Thus this collection is at one level a modest set of practical ideas for implementing Design and Technology in primary school classrooms, and other early childhood settings. Nonetheless, the underlying position is far from modest. Giving children a sense that they can control their environment, and a sense of both the possibilities of, and the limitations on, that control, is an important justification for starting to implement primary school Design and Technology as soon as possible.

It is of course, not only the children who need a sense that they are in control of things. If teachers are to be freed of some of the uncertainty they feel about primary school Design and Technology, they too have to discover a sense of being in control of it. We hope that the articles in this volume will make a contribution to this end.

References

[1] Department of Education and Science (1978) *Primary Education in England; a survey by HMI.* HMSO.

[2] Department of Education and Science (1989) *Standards in Education.* HMSO.

[3] Department of Education and Science (1987) *The National Curriculum; a consultation document.* HMSO.

[4] Department of Education and Science (1988) *National Curriculum, Design and Technology Working Group, Interim Report.* HMSO.

[5] Wragg, E, Bennett, N., and Carre, C. (1989) 'Teachers' Worries over National Curriculum Revealed,' *Junior Education,* June. Leamington Spa, Scholastic Books.

[6] Department of Education and Science (1988) *1987 Primary Staffing Survey, List of Tables.* HMSO.

[7] Department of Education and Science (1989) *National Curriculum, Design and Technology Working Group, Final Report.* HMSO.

DESIGN AND TECHNOLOGY: ploughing through the paper

Mike Sullivan

What's in a name?

I was beginning to get used to CDT, my lad took it at the comp. It was woodwork and metalwork and making his initials out of pink plastic. I could cope with that. The one-up brigade in the local primaries described the models that children knocked up in project work as CDT. I could cope with that too. As a fairly practical feet-on-the-ground sort I have a feeling for craft; making, doing and knowing just about describes my sort of teaching. *National Curriculum Design and Technology Working Group: Interim Report*[1] and *Design and Technology for ages 5 to 16*[2] came as a bit of a shock. From CDT to DT did this mean no making and no doing? All concepts and attitudes but no skills? This doesn't sound quite my sort of thing. I could see myself having problems with the staff too. I could persuade some one to have maths, science, music or PE but to have DT? Isn't DT about seeing pink elephants after drinking too much? Is it possible to plan for Design and Technology without taking skills into account? How is the investigation in Design and Technology different to the investigation in science? It was time to do some investigating into the documents on my own account.

The Curriculum Matters Series

My starting point is *The Curriculum from 5 to 16*[3]. No mention of CDT or DT in the nine areas of learning or experience but 'aesthetic and creative' and 'technological' appear.

'[The area of aesthetic and creative] is concerned with the capacity to respond emotionally to sensory experience; the awareness of degrees of quality; and the appreciation of beauty and fitness for purpose .... Art, crafts, design, some aspects of technology, music, dance, drama and theatre arts, in particular, promote the development of the imagination and the creative use of media and materials.'   (p 17)

There doesn't seem to be anything to object to there even though it sounds a bit woolly so it must be an aim rather than an objective. It all gets a bit tighter a little later on:

'Through drawing, painting, modelling, carving, designing and constructing, pupils should acquire knowledge and skills and develop perceptions which enable them to make a personal response to what they see, touch and feel. Primary age children can begin to consider the importance of the choice of medium in creating a particular effect, while older pupils may examine the relationship between aesthetics and fitness for purpose in design. (p 17)

It certainly looks as if HMI are on the reassuringly familiar tack of placing practical experience first and they also make the point that fitness for purpose in design comes high up the hierarchy of educational objectives.

HMI don't quite at this stage give a definition of technology but say that:

'The essence of technology lies in the process of bringing about change or exercising control over the environment. The process is a particular form of problem solving: of designing in order to effect control.'   (p 34)

This seems fairly clear but in the very next paragraph I'm thrown into confusion:

'Young children can be brought to understand that, while steel is hard, it is also elastic; that glass is not only brittle but strong; that some materials deform irrevocably when stretched while others regain their former shape; that some materials change their characteristics when heated.'

Is this not the sort of physical science that we have been engaged in for years?'

'Pupils need to learn that these characteristics are important when it comes to choosing materials for the solution of particular problems.'

This is a qualifier that offers little help; physical science has never been taught in an academic vacuum in primary schools, it has always been related to the world around us.

The problems of being the most gullible man in the world are many. I do accept, in great innocence and trust, that those wiser and better than me are acting with the purest of motives. Yet I begin to have a nagging suspicion that the disappearance of craft is some mechanism for avoiding discussion about resource implications.

The omnibus *Design and Technology for ages 5 to 16*[2] includes the design and technological areas to be found in 'art and design, business studies, CDT, home economics and information technology'. *Home Economics from 5 to 16*[4] defines the primary aim of teaching home economics in school as:

'to help prepare boys and girls for some important aspects of everyday living and the adult responsibilities of family life ... although theory and knowledge are important in developing such competences, they should be related closely to the performance of practical tasks.'   (p 1)

In the 36 page document of approximately fourteen thousand words 'design' or 'designing' is used eleven times and 'technology' or 'technological' appears on six occasions.

Certainly HMI in 1985 were not seeing 'Home Economics' as having much to do with design and technology but were certainly seeing it as a 'making and doing' curriculum area.

Craft, Design and Technology from 5 to 16[5] begins with an attempt to define CDT:

'The purpose of CDT is to enable pupils to be inventive in designing practical solutions to problems and so to bring about change and improvements in existing situations. In CDT ideas are conceived, developed, modified and given shape in artefacts through which the original ideas can then be evaluated.

In CDT **design** involves designing a task, deciding on how a task is to be done and responding to the consequences of thoughts and actions both as they happen and later when the result is judged. It is directed towards products or systems which are made or effected to meet specified requirements.'   (p 1)

Technology is seen in terms of the application of knowledge and experience.

'It is concerned with controlling things or making things work better.'   (p 2)

The definition goes on to add:

'Children's early attempts at using or re-arranging materials to make things are within that tradition; as is their increasing ability to succeed in putting their ideas into practice.'

There is also a definition of craft:

'Craft is the means through which designs are transformed into artefacts. Through a proper concern for craftsmanship, people make things which not only work well but which also look and feel attractive. Craft skills need to be acquired because, without them, pupils can become frustrated by their inability to produce that which, in their imagination, works perfectly and looks and feels pleasing.'   (p 2)

An important feature of CDT for HMI is that design and technology are being constantly interwoven:

'craft skills are learnt and practised in response to the demands of a particular design or to the choice of a certain technology. A pupil's design may be developed or modified to suit his/her level of craftsmanship or a different technology may be substituted which removes the need for very advanced technical skills.'   (p 2)

Information Technology 5 to 16 (Curriculum Matters 15)[6] takes on a wider brief than that given to the Design and Technology Curriculum Working Group of the National Curriculum.

Information Technology is defined as:

'the technology associated with the handling of information: its storage, possessing and transmission in a variety of forms by electronic means, and its use in controlling the operations of machines and other devices.'   (p 1)

HMI sound words of warning about training needs and shortage of equipment. They also sharply underline the unequal distribution of resources and expertise (p 9). This is worth underlining for the problem of adequately resourcing all schools is one of increasing difficulty. Funding schools through LMS is likely to cause even greater inequalities. Larger schools serving prosperous areas are likely to end up with a far greater number of modern machines through money raised in the community and the way in which formula funding will be operated. Those children in disadvantaged areas are likely to have less access time in that the ratio of pupils to machines will be poorer and they will be less likely to have access to computers in the home. Schools serving disadvantaged areas will also have problems in the up-dating of expensive resources in a rapidly developing technology.

HMI identify general objectives for IT, with six topics and 'related objectives' for each in the primary curriculum. It is interesting to observe how tenuous the links are between IT and Design and Technology.

Communicating ideas and information

a. understand the ways in which a word processor can help in planning and undertaking a writing task;
b. be sufficiently familiar and adept with the standard keyboard to enable them effectively to translate ideas into text, and to produce a piece of work using such editing facilities as insertion, deletion and movement of text.
c. be able to rework their writing showing a sensitive awareness of readership, purpose and potential of the medium;
d. understand that the choice and order of words and illustrations, the format and size of text and graphics affect readability and impact. (p 11)

Information handling

a. know that computer based information may exist in different forms (text, numbers, graphics);
b. be able to extract and display information in different ways from data previously stored by themselves or others;
c. understand the need to question the reliability of displayed information and the fact that results produced by a computer may be influenced by the incorrect entry of data;
d. be able to interpret processed data and examine its plausibility;
e. be able to design a simple structure within which a limited set of data may be captured, stored and retrieved;
f. be able to interrogate data to examine patterns and relationships in the information and to form and test simple hypotheses. (p 13)

IT representations of real or imaginary situations and mathematical calculations

a. understand that a computer may simulate a situation by following a set of rules consistently, although sometimes random events may be incorporated;
b. understand that computer simulations are not complete and accurate representations of reality;
c. understand that a computer is able to act on a sequence of instructions from a user and that such a sequence may be stored;
d. be able to participate effectively in collaborative decision making, whether as a leader or as a team member;
e. be able to recognise when the use of an electronic calculator or computer is appropriate to the mathematical task in hand and be able to handle it competently. (p 14)

The aesthetic aspect of the curriculum

a. be able to create and store pieces of visual imagery and/or sound compositions;
b. be able to access and re-work existing sounds or images to produce controlled results which express their ideas;
c. be able to use IT sensitively in relation to different viewers or audiences.   (p 16)

Designing, making, measuring and controlling in the physical environment

a. understand from personal experience that certain toys, switches, domestic appliances and computers can respond to given signals or commands;
b. understand that a computer can control devices by means of a series of commands, and appreciate the need for precision in the framing of such commands;
c. know from personal experience that environmental changes can be detected, measured and responded to, particularly in domestic appliances or scientific measurements;
d. be able to construct a working model which responds only to certain environmental conditions;
e. be able to build a set of commands (a procedure) to control the movement of a screen image or a robot in an effective manner.   (p 17)

Some consequences of IT for society and the individual

a. know about everyday jobs which make use of IT;
b. know about types of information of interest to themselves and their families which may be held on computers;
c. be able to identify particular effects that a new or different IT application has had on themselves, their families or the community;
d. understand that technological developments have both advantages and disadvantages. (p 18)

National Curriculum Design and Technology Working Group: creativity by numbers?

The terms of reference of the Working Group instructed them to view technology as 'that area of the curriculum in which pupils design and make useful objects or systems, thus developing their ability to solve practical problems.' Certainly there is a recognition that children will need to be 'making and doing', though quality through craftsmanship seems to be a missing element at this stage. Technology is seen as a subject in its own right, with its own distinctive objectives and content but also seen as going 'across the curriculum' drawing on and linking with a wide

range of subjects.

The Interim Report[1] produced by the Working Group in November 1988 proposed just one profile component for Design and Technology which was named 'design and technological capability'. This profile component was linked to five attainment targets.

Design and Technology Attainment Targets Proposed in the Interim Report

AT1
Explore and investigate contexts for design and technological capabilities

AT2
Formulate proposals and choose a design for development

AT3
Develop the design and plan for the making of an artefact or system

AT4
Make artefacts and systems

AT5
Appraise the processes, outcomes and effects of design and technological activities

The Working Group was concerned that what it was advocating might wrongly be interpreted as a 'skills-led' as opposed to a 'knowledge-led' approach. It argued that skills were always dependent on knowledge (p 74). This seems something of a 'straw man' for at least those of us in primary schools are committed to an 'activity' based approach - believing that both skills and knowledge grow out of purposeful activity.

I have long suspected that one of the purposes of recent legislation is to make illegal, fun and enjoyment in learning and teaching. To change state education into commercial and industrial training. The language and content of the Design and Technology reports do nothing to dispel my suspicions. The Interim Report and all other NC reports seem devoid of references to such terms as pleasure, leisure and self-fulfilment. Perhaps, for some, the 'craft' in CDT conjures up visions of weaving, pottery and pipe racks. Too soft and civilised for the present political climate geared to thrusting commercial entrepreneurism.

The Interim Report defends the change from CDT to DT in the following way:

'It might be objected that a more appropriate title would be 'Craft, Design and Technology' which is already widely used in secondary schools. However, while CDT has much to contribute, we are dealing with an activity broader than CDT which, to quote our terms of reference, 'goes across the curriculum, drawing on and linking with a wide range of subjects.' (p 74)

Although the Working Group provided general guidance for Information Technology in the Interim Report it was unable at that stage to identify possible attainment targets.

Design and Technology for ages 5 to 16 – Final Report

The first obvious difference between the interim and final[2] proposals of the Working Group is the collapse from the initial five attainment targets to four in the Design and Technology profile component. The second difference is the introduction of an Information Technology profile component.

Design and Technology Attainment Targets Final Report

AT1
Identifying Needs and Opportunities

Through exploration and investigation of a range of contexts (home; school; recreation; community; business and industry) pupils should be able to identify and state clearly needs and opportunities for design and technological activities.

This attainment target has changed little in passage from interim to final report.

AT2
Generating a Design Proposal

Pupils should be able to produce a realistic, appropriate and achievable design by generating, exploring and developing design and technological ideas and by refining and detailing the design proposal they have chosen.

The content of this attainment target again has changed little.

AT3
Planning and Making

Working to a plan derived from their previously developed design, pupils should be able to identify, manage and use appropriate resources, including both knowledge and processes in order to make an artefact, system or environment.

The compression of the planning and making process into a single attainment target throws again into question the value given to making.

AT4
Appraising

Pupils should be able to develop, communicate and act constructively upon an appraisal of the processes, outcomes and effects of their own design and technological activity as well as of the outcomes and effects of the design and technological activity of others, including those from other times and cultures.

A welcome addition to the attainment target is the recognition that other cultures can make a contribution to understanding of technology. However, the guidance given (paras. 1.44 to 1.46) is of little practical use.

Information technology

The final report is still less than convincing in its claim that IT is any more an essential part of technology and design than that of any other curriculum area. Assurances are given that the differences in equipment levels in schools have been taken into account. With many primary schools having more classes than computers, it is difficult to see how children are going to follow the example given for Level 3 and 'draft a diary of a school visit' without some children having to wait for a very long time. Even with the luxury of one computer per class it is difficult for children to obtain worthwhile keyboard experience.

Changing aims? Changing objectives? Changing delivery?

The final report reminds us that much teaching at Key Stages 1 and 2 is presently based on themes and topics, eg transport, my body, weather, road safety, castles, flight. The Working Group assumes that this general pattern of curriculum organisation will continue and that the 'matters', knowledge and skills in the relevant programmes of study are delivered mainly through such topics. (p 86) Hang on! What's happened to the holy trinity of 'attitudes, knowledge and skills'? What's the difference between 'matters' and 'knowledge' — does is matter anyway?

Cynics may be forgiven for assuming that all they need to do is keep the title the same but give the actiivities alternative titles.

Later on the same page we are told that

'It will also be necessary for one teacher to have responsibility of co-ordinating the work of the whole school, including the use of resources, and provide assistance to other teachers.' (p 1)

A neat trick if you can manage it but most of us in schools will either ignore this recommendation or give the hard pressed teacher responsible for science this extra responsibility too. If this is so then technology is likely to be subsumed under the umbrella of physical science and one of the major points of the exercise is almost entirely lost.

The distinction between science and technology is further eroded when looking at the proposed programme of study for level 1 (p 25) where, under the heading of 'Social and Environmental' pupils should be taught to 'talk about the needs of people, animals and plants'. At level 1 children should also be taught to 'recognise, handle and use safely a variety of simple tools'. I'm not too sure as to what is being suggested here as a sledge hammer and an axe are very simple tools whilst a hole punch represents much more sophisticated technology! Far more useful is the advice given in *Science in Primary Schools*[7] which lists a suitable range of tools and other equipment that children and teachers would find useful in the classroom.

The final report looks at the ways in which assessment should take place. The advice is rather sketchy in emphasising that technology integrates exploring, modelling, appraising and that these processes are continuously interacting with each other. Any assessment should not distort the nature of the activity and that 'there are always several possible solutions to a design and technology task.' (p 82 para. 4.6)

The specific advice on internal assessment given to primary teachers is less than helpful.

'Most primary teachers are well used to project work. The main challenges to teachers at this level will be to identify the design and technological aspects of pupils' work and to observe carefully the progress which individual pupils are making and keep systematic records of their assessments.' (p 83 4.17)'

There are difficulties in making value judgements about 'right answers' to problems. If pupils turn up the 'sledgehammer to crack a nut' solution to a problem — a solution that is reliable but crude is this more valuable than a solution that doesn't work but incorporates novel ideas and a very high level of sophistication?

It is also very difficult to assess an individual's contribution to a group solution. I can't ever recollect seeing convincing records of individual pupils' achievements in topic work.

It might have all the lights, bells and buzzers but will it work?

The answer is yes, for the documents do provide a rough sieve which helps us in primary schools identify the presence or absence of technological content in the work that we prepare for children.

All children are entitled to a balanced curriculum which includes a practical understanding of some technological principles. With any luck these principles will help us capture the imagination of some children and excite them with wonder in the magic of technology. Have you ever wondered why the quartz in a digital watch vibrates at a constant rate and how they make the numbers change and how they can sell it for £1.99 at the local garage and still make a profit?

References

[1] DES (1988) *National Curriculum Design and Technology Working Group, Interim Report.* HMSO.

[2] DES (1989) *Design and Technology for ages 5 to 16.* HMSO.

[3] DES (1985) *The Curriculum from 5 to 16: Curriculum Matters 2.* HMSO.

[4] DES (1985) *Home Economics from 5 to 16: Curriculum Matters 5.* HMSO.

[5] DES (1987) *Craft, Design and Technology from 5 to 16: Curriculum Matters 9.* HMSO.

[6] DES (1989) *Information Technology from 5 to 16: Curriculum Matters 15.* HMSO.

[7] DES (1983) *Science in Primary Schools.* A discussion paper produced by the HMI Science Committee. HMSO.

WHO'S AFRAID OF CDT?

Rod Bosanko   *deputy head, Shirley Heath Junior School, Solihull*

Current Conceptions of CDT

The new band wagon in primary education is Craft Design and Technology. Before it gets too much momentum, we should hold it still to examine more closely what it is that we are being encouraged to jump up on. Current conceptions about CDT in primary schools appear to have derived from secondary curriculum practice, for it often seems to be presented in ways that make it easy to think of it as a separate 'subject', or as part of Science.

For example, despite their broad conception of CDT as a problem-solving activity applicable across the curriculum, in *The Curriculum From 5 to 16* HMI present it in the following terms (para 74):

> 'Subjects (sic) such as home economics and CDT enable pupils to apply and investigate scientific principles . . .'

And (in para 83/84) in discussing what HMI call the technological area of experience, there is almost what amounts to a call for CDT to have a separate curricular existence, equal to other more conventional curriculum subjects.

> 'Learning about technology and its historical and social consequences and exploring the opportunities to apply scientific principles that involvement with it makes possible, have long featured in the work of schools. Such work should continue and, if anything, be increased in scale and range. But work of that kind does not of itself make up a technological area of learning and experience sufficiently delineated and comprehensive to stand alongside the other, more firmly established, areas that should feature in a broad curriculum. The study of the impact of technology and its social and environmental 'spin-offs', however interesting, is no substitute for active involvement in the process itself.
>
> All pupils throughout the 5 – 16 period should be so involved. The essence of technology lies in the process of bringing about change or exercising control over the environment. This process is a particular form of problem solving: of designing in order to effect control. It is common to all technologies including those concerned with the provision of shelter, food, clothing, methods of maintaining health or communicating with others, and also with the so-called high technologies of electronics, biotechnology and fuel extraction and the alternative technologies of the Third World. As in all learning, the involvement must be characterised by progression, internal coherence and continuity. But technology also has its content which, while not exclusive to it, is essential to the technological process. That content broadly concerns the nature and characteristics of natural and manufactured materials, and the nature, control and transformation of energy.'

Strictly speaking, of course, 'areas of experience' are not 'subjects', but the problem with presenting the case for CDT as a distinctive area of the curriculum, linked to science, is that the response of many primary school teachers is likely to be negative. They may well react to HMI proposals much as they did to Science in the 1970s – with a sense of both fear and professional incompetence, except that this time there is the further problem that teachers will see it as one more subject which they have to incorporate unresourced, into an already overcrowded timetable, or as just one additional burden to all the new priorities (SEN, multi-culturalism, diagnostic assessment, micro-computer applications, able children etc) currently hovering over them.

CDT as an Approach to Learning

This reaction, though understandable, would be a pity. For years many primary school teachers have been involved in CDT to some extent, perhaps without realising it. We have worked with our children in groups as they have identified problems, posed solutions and tested them through designing, making and evaluating models which illustrate their investigations, in history, geography, mathematics, art craft and language. The value of these models has been immense not only for the children who have made them but also for those who have seen them on display. It is this experience that could be built on to extend CDT in primary schools. This view of CDT, an approach to learning across the curriculum characterised by co-operative group work, exploratory language focussed on defining problems, model making to test possible solutions, and appraisal of results, is not new. It was advocated as a learning approach by Plowden in 1967. And that is its advantage. It starts from where many teachers already are. Primary school teachers could come to realise that they have been 'doing CDT' to some extent already, and can extend it simply by reflecting upon the possibilities for practical problem solving in more curriculum areas.

The practical aspect of actually asking children to work in groups to discuss ideas, identify problems, decide upon an approach, to draw preliminary plans, to collect all their materials, to construct a model from their initial plans and to evaluate how their final model has differed from their original idea, is the vital progression of a whole range of theoretical, practical and co-operative skills. It is important for the children to draw plans of the finished item and then to write notes illustrating and highlighting any difficulties that arose and explaining how their ideas might have changed as practical problems were overcome. This is the precise procedure in miniature followed by those in industry who innovate and improve.

In this way, a model of say a Norman Castle could pose problems of structure and stability, measurement and calculation, design and construction. It could lead on to work on patterns of bricklaying which can make strong walls and arches, and a whole range of investigations into building techniques ancient and modern. In addition, the construction of a seige machine will introduce children to projectiles and at this point you would probably have to decide whether or not to forget the Normans and follow the natural curiosity of the children and widen your work to study flight.

Admittedly CDT in its present widely accepted sense is much less of a problem for the teacher who has some experience in science, as by its very nature it is practical and relies to an extent upon scientific principles, but this emphasis is restricting. Micro-computers were initially regarded as a tool for the mathematician until it was accepted that they had a wider use across the curriculum. So too, with CDT. It is not something which stands on its own but rather extends into most subjects and is the tool whereby investigations or demonstrations of ideas are made possible. It it probably one of the highest order problem solving activities in which children can engage. The interest is self-generating and the match between the individual's ability and the work she or he is doing is high.

The Development of CDT in my Class

The work in my own school went through two stages; that in my own classroom and that done by other teachers in response to my suggestion that we organise a CDT exhibition in the school.

As the teacher responsible for CDT in the school, I had successfully negotiated with the local authority inspectors some help in providing a basic tool kit, some of it redeployed from secondary schools. And my head had let me spend a further £400 on material from catalogues. Parents responded keenly to requests for raw materials, as did one or two local firms, and the local hospital. From these community sources, I finished up with amongst other things, a ready supply of:

old clocks for the gears, old radios for the on/off switches, rheostats, speakers, old spectacles for the lenses, coffee jar lids – to make excellent wheels, knitting needles – to make excellent axles, injection syringes – to make hydraulic systems, and so on.

By this means, I had created a resource base for the work.

In my own class of top juniors, my basic aims are to give children a sense of control over technology/science/the social world, by giving them the responsibility for identifying their own problems, and arriving at solutions. For this reason, I did not, and do not, have a written syllabus or scheme. If this happens, it means that there is a 'correct' answer somewhere in the back of the teacher's mind. Also I want to allow my children the privilege of embarking upon an idea that we can see may lead nowhere. But because the children are able to argue well that they should pursue that particular avenue, they themselves must reach the decision that their original assumption was wrong. It has to be monitored carefully, of course, and skilled guidance must be given so that valuable time and enthusiasm are not wasted; when children realise that they are up in blind alley, I have to be ready to step in, resume and redirect their energy, interest and enthusiasm. The ability to tolerate ambiguity is a pre-requisite for high level problem solving, and therefore I as a teacher have to be working and learning with the children as an integral member of the design team, rather than an overseer or director.

My basic classroom organisation is very flexible. Apart from time set aside for Maths and English, the rest of the time is divided up between PE, TV, and what I call Research. Over the year this covers a wide curricular range, and always includes language, mathematics, history, geography, art and craft. This time is used to develop topics that have arisen from some other aspect of the children's work, and at any one time you might find a group writing poetry, drawing detailed plans, reading for pleasure, writing up an experiment, painting, or many other things.

A key characteristic of most group activities is a problem solving approach, related to the work they are doing. I always allow a group to select itself around a point of interest. They discuss and identify a problem, and postulate theories as to its possible solution. They become a design team.

One such group was working on a project on Transport which, as a spin-off considered cars as transport and as performance vehicles. I involved myself early on:

'O.K. These cars use petrol, but I wonder if it is possible for you to build a vehicle which will travel more than 1 metre under its own power. You can't shove it or roll it down a slope. You must let it go from a standing start.'

Much pencil sucking goes on for about half an hour. Soon diagrams appear on scraps of paper. An argument about a power unit occurs. Other children are drawn in. There are two schools of thought. One favours elastic bands and the other favours electric motors. More pencil sucking, more plans, more arguments. Another split is occurring. Someone wants to use jet power, and they think a balloon will do. Eventually there are five distinct design teams discussing, exchanging ideas in a sort of mutual guarded secrecy because they want to have the winning design.

The designs are shown to me and with one or two suggestions they have my blessing to proceed. After weeks of trial, re-design, improvement, wonderful use of language both spoken and written, mathematical calculations and measurement, interaction within a group, modifications, trials of theories based on scientific ideas and knowledge, we had a variety of vehicles.

There was a basic four wheel drive car powered by an elastic band. But the children wanted to improve its performance. They found out that to 'triangulate' the elastic band gave more power, but to do this they had to build a stable rectangular frame, (see Fig. 2.3.1).

This diagram shows the solution that one group of 'average' children arrived at after a great deal of trial and error, dogged perseverance, and downright hard work. They had had to overcome friction in the axles, and turn the energy provided by the elastic bands through 90° to power the back wheels. They had to solve problems of stability and rigidity as well as a whole range of other difficulties that they encountered.

An interesting discussion arose in this group regarding the numbers of teeth on different cogs, which developed into a peripheral study on gear ratios. The children created experiments for themselves with cogs where they investigated how many teeth were on this or that cog, and how many times it went round when driven by the first cog. There was even a rather optimistic discussion on whether or not to try to develop a gearbox to make the car go even faster, but at this point the children realised their own limitations. What had happened, however was that their eyes had been opened to a new dimension of experience, and although they had no immediate practical solution to their problem, they had been engaged in postulating theories, and in exploring the problem through intellectual reasoning.

When they returned to the task in hand, a more basic but nevertheless important intuitive modification was made, where they decided to put sandpaper on the rear wheels to increase friction with the floor because when they gave the elastic 20 turns the back wheels spun and that was a waste of energy.

Because the car travelled in a curve, some other children tried a rudimentary form of steering based on a 3 wheeled vehicle which they thought would go further because it was lighter. It did, and it went in a straight line.

The balloon powered cars just managed to travel one metre, but only when someone discovered that if you put a button in the neck of the balloon, you restrict the emission of air and increase the duration of the thrust. They also discovered inertia because the vehicle kept moving after the balloon had gone down.

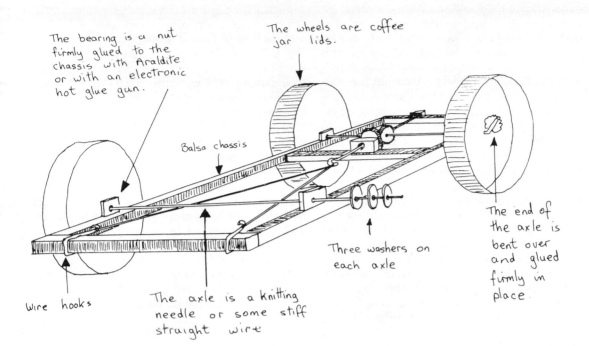

The bearing is a nut firmly glued to the chassis with Araldite or with an electronic hot glue gun.

The wheels are coffee jar lids.

Balsa chassis

The end of the axle is bent over and glued firmly in place.

Wire hooks

The axle is a knitting needle or some stiff straight wire

Three washers on each axle

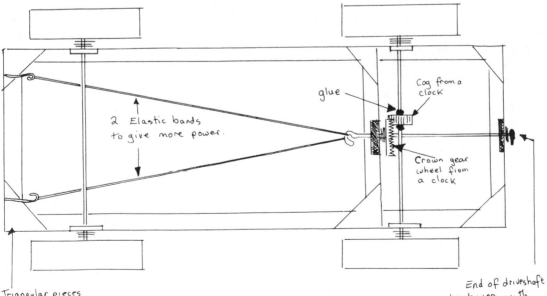

2 Elastic bands to give more power.

glue

Cog from a clock

Crown gear wheel from a clock

Triangular pieces of card glued on to give added strength

End of driveshaft bent over with a blob of glue on it to keep the washers in place.

Fig. 2.3.1
Diagram for a Four-Wheel Drive Car

The electric motor powered cars ran by (a) rubbing the motor spindle on the back wheel (b) using an elastic band in the same way as a bicycle chain. (c) using gears taken from clocks.

One group wanted forward and reverse and stop without having to fiddle around with changing wires. They wired up a household two way lighting switch themselves! The electric cars, the children decided, would go as long as the batteries would allow them to, so how were they to choose the best car? One of the children, considered least able in conventional terms, suggested building a ramp out of a plank on bricks and gradually increasing the slope.

This posed new challenges for them. They too put sandpaper on the wheels, experimented with centre of gravity to stop the cars flipping over and so on. Eventually, a girl and a boy came up with the best design: a four wheel drive electric powered car with forward, reverse and stop, together with a variable speed control (this was a volume control from an old tape recorder) which would climb a slope of 41°. I wonder if Range Rover can match that!

Developing CDT Through the School

It was relatively easy for me to develop the approach in my own class. But what about other classes in the school? I had to motivate them. They had been aware that something peculiar had been going on in my room, because occasionally things whirred down the corridor or flew through the air, or buzzed or chimed. Strange machines were being made and tested.

I went to the teachers, in turn, and discussed with them what work they would be doing next term, and carefully raised with them some possibilities for building in a more explicit problem solving approach. In our staff meeting I threw out what I now realise was a bombshell.

'How about us all getting as much CDT work as possible out of our topics, and let's share a CDT exhibition in the school?'

Stony silence!

But I urged them to do it, pointing out examples across the curriculum:

Art: colours, the eye, lenses, chromotography, dyes, etc.
History: Great inventors and designers such as Archimedes, Newton, Da Vinci, Flight, Boats, Cars and improvements in the designs.
Drama: Create a stage in a cardboard box, use puppets and light it with torchbulbs and switches.

In short, I asked the staff to think of their own strengths, to come to me with their topics, and see how we could plan to integrate the CDT approach into them. I argued that they should see CDT as an 'enabler', an approach that would enable them and their children to extend their existing work by improving the quality of its problem solving potential. And they agreed, some with more silent reservations than I knew at the time. But once committed to an open week exhibition, they responded positively, and some examples of their work illustrate how well 'non-specialists' can add new dimensions to their work through CDT.

A class of first year juniors (Y3) had begun some work on food and were investigating crops and diet and so on, when one girl decided that she wanted to make a model of a windmill. The teacher expected the model to be the usual box with some sails stuck on the front, but the little girl wanted more than that. She decided that she wanted to wind a handle at the back and make the sails go round. The teacher gave her all the support and confidence she needed but when the model was complete, she still wasn't satisfied.

In her mind she had a picture of her model looking and functioning like a real windmill. She cut the side out of the windmill and made cogs out of cotton reels with lolly sticks stuck into them. She put in a vertical driveshaft which had two more cotton reels at the bottom representing the millstones. There were three floors inside her windmill complete with storage bins, sacks, with real corn, and sacks with real flour in them. There was a miller and his cat and a whole range of tools and milling equipment.

When the handle was turned, the sails went round, the top millstone turned and some flour which had been carefully put into the top cotton reel trickled out from between the millstones.

The model was a joy to see especially when you realised the range of skills that the little girl had experienced. She had researched her ideas from books and a visit to a water powered mill, and modified her model according to the materials which were available to her. She was evaluating her ideas and theories and was developing them into real problem solving areas. She was communicating her ideas and enthusiasm to others not only in what she was making, writing and drawing, but in what she was saying.

As a direct result of her enthusiasm and her teacher's skill and ability to recognise a new and exciting area of work, other children became interested in cogs and pulleys, and a whole range of experiments sprang up which investigated energy transfer. Children worked in self-selected groups and they nailed cotton reels into pieces of wood and looped elastic bands around them. When one cotton reel was turned, they all turned. Some went forwards and some went backwards and the children found out why for themselves. Other children used crown caps from beer bottles in the same way except that the wavy edges of the caps interlocked like cogs. Not only did this work provide the children with an enormous practical experience, but these models made superb kinetic pictures on the wall. The scientific and aesthetic came together for a class of 7–8 year-olds. (I don't think they were ever separate in the first place although I am sure there are many who will dispute that point.)

Fortunately the class teacher concerned was flexible enough in his ideas to realise the potential of this work and to have the courage to change direction rather than to doggedly stick to his original scheme of work. The children gained much experience in mechanics, language, art, mathematics, geography, history, manipulative and practical skills and so on. Eventually the work became a study of energy in its various forms and it enhanced the original idea of food, which is after all one of our own prime sources of energy.

Another class which was involved with some work on art diversified into the study of colour. They investigated how paints mixed and compared the results with the way light mixes. They split white light into the spectrum of colours and then tried to re-mix those colours using spinning tops with the 7 segments coloured in. The work developed into chromatography and then to a study of the eye which led on to work on lenses. Using the information they were gaining the children developed their work in groups into making simple telescopes, cameras and optical toys.

There were numerous other examples. Perhaps one of the most interesting pieces of work was done by a second year (Y4) class who were considering space. Not outer space, but inner space. The space between objects, people and events. Space within structures, creatures, music, poetry, maths and art and so on. And there was the music topic in which the children's creativity led them to invent and play their own musical instruments and to discover the connection between frequency and pitch. A first year (Y3)

class working on a maths project concerned with time came up with fascinating ways of measuring time and subsequently wrote and performed a marvellous assembly about it.

Conclusion

The CDT exhibition in the school was a great success; the school opened itself up to its public for a week, with each class supplying, on a rota, a team of 'boffins' to demonstrate its displays, and to talk about the work. Everyone in each class, irrespective of ability, had a turn at being boffin, and did the job with enthusiasm and pride. Our visitors included parents and other members of the community, the local press, advisers and inspectors, and education officers. They found enthusiastic children, anxious to share their learning with them, by showing them how things worked, and how some other things worked even better!

Behind these public scenes, something else had happened. The staff as a whole had grasped the nettle and created an extended dimension to their curriculum practice. For me this was best illustrated by one of my colleagues, a first year (Y3) teacher who had found the approach rather challenging but at the same time exhilarating. Emerging from her classroom one day as the exhibition's opening day approached, her arms full of pictures, models, plans, writing etc, to be displayed in the corridor, she saw me passing by.

'Oh, I have had a good day, and just look at all the work they've done for me!'

What I look for in the future, is not a wrangle between polarised factions in education, arguing about whose definition of CDT will be the dominant one. Instead, I hope that primary school classteachers, perhaps with a little help from their technically-minded friends, will come to see the potential for their normal work that resides in the movement for CDT. For it could be the best thing to come their way in a long time. Through the kind of approach I have been illustrating, we can go some way to reclaiming what used to be called 'progressivism'. We can demonstrate that children's learning does not proceed through adult notions of 'subjects', and can implement a problem-solving approach to learning across the curriculum that stresses children's definitions and children's solutions.

CRAFT DESIGN TECHNOLOGY IN THE PRIMARY SCHOOL: let's keep it primary

Iain Milloy   *advisory teacher, Birmingham LEA*

What's in a name?

The obvious answer must be that it depends on the name! Take 'Craft Design Technology'. Among teachers this title conjures up a wide range of impressions . . . and prejudices. Now link 'CDT' with primary education – particularly across the Infant years – and you will certainly provoke from primary teachers some interesting responses.

Many teachers will state that they do not know what CDT really means. They will point out, however, that CDT 'sounds' very secondary . . . very male-orientated; that it must be a highly specialist subject that requires extensive, 'hi-tech' resources.

Some teachers will welcome the practical nature of CDT with its emphasis upon learning through direct experience. Yet, they have considerable reservations about their competence to manage the 'teaching' requirements of CDT. Furthermore, they may feel wary of committing themselves and their children to a 'subject' that appears to lack a clear structure and well-marked routes of progression.

Not surprisingly, there are teachers who have been encouraging CDT-style activities with their children, but who have been completely unaware that they were 'doing' CDT!

The most immediate response to these comments must be that many teachers have difficulty in reconciling their impressions of CDT with everyday experience of primary education.

So where does this semantic investigation lead? Two basic conclusions emerge:

(a)   the title 'CDT' must be recognised as a very heavily-charged term that can cause a great deal of confusion and prejudice among teachers – to the disadvantage of children;

(b)   there is an urgent need to offer primary teachers a 'working definition' of CDT–style activities as a necessary prelude to promoting primary CDT.

What is CDT?

Most teachers would initially assume that CDT is a subject, or an amalgam of subjects based, for instance, upon craft and science. The essence of CDT, however, does not lie in any specific combination of subjects. CDT is an approach to learning. It represents a commitment to the value for children of learning through genuine problem-solving experience.

CDT in action reflects the general characteristics of any problem-solving activity, eg a realistic situation in which children recognise a need and identify a problem, the application of a range of problem-solving strategies set within a 'team context', and the evaluation of a 'solution'. Yet, CDT introduces a distinctive element into this experience for the children through the intensely practical and 'immediate' nature of the problem and possible solutions: children use simple materials, tools and equipment to produce their solutions. The moving force behind CDT is, however, the conviction that, when sensitively guided by the teacher, problem-solving engages children in highly relevant learning experieces:experiences that have an enabling influence upon the intellectual, practical, personal and social development of children.

There can be little doubt that the principles underlying CDT are in full sympathy with the major aims and objectives of primary education. Yet, the move from principles into practice is not so straightforward. The basic challenge at primary level lies in the promotion of a genuinely primary orientation to CDT-style activities.

This challenge breaks down into at least five basic requirements:

(a) Primary CDT must evolve from a foundation of 'good' primary practice. It cannot, and must not, take root as a secondary transplant. If it is a valid form of problem-solving experience at primary level, it must have direct relevance across the full primary age and ability range – and, in addition, carry no taint of male bias. Consequently, the development of primary CDT should not be allowed to be dominated and moulded by impressions of secondary practice. (This does not deny the urgent need for thorough liaison between primary and secondary CDT.)

(b) CDT-style activities must be manageable for the 'generalist' teacher.

(c) The activities themselves must be capable of accomodation within the general-purpose classroom.

(d) CDT-style activities must not be dependent upon specialist or 'hi-tech' resources.

(e) Appropriate INSET provision must be made to help teachers develop greater awareness, confidence and competence in respect of CDT.

These requirements raise complex issues, but this article, however, focuses upon some of those connected with the first four points.

First of all, back to semantics! The term, 'Craft Design Technology', is not particulary teacher friendly. It lacks primary appeal. This dissatisfaction with 'CDT' is not new. Other titles have been proposed. Probably the most effective alternative is quite simply, 'Designing and Making.'

As a title, 'Designing and Making' has distinct merits:

– It 'sounds' primary. It has no secondary or specialist overtones. It avoids any obvious pressure for 'hi-tech' activities. It is reasonably gender-neutral.

– The leading word, 'Designing', stresses the thinking or problem-solving character of the experience for children. Moreover, it links the 'Making' directly with problem-solving as the means of expressing the solution.

– 'Making' underlines the practical, physical nature of this activity. The simplicity of the term, 'Making', is particularly fortunate since it relates very easily to the resources, activities and general scenario in primary classrooms, from Nursery and Reception through to Top Junior.

From this point onwards, 'Designing and Making' will be used in preference to 'CDT'.

How does this view of Designing and Making fit in with the realities of teaching?

'We go to be talked to by unbelievably enthusiastic and terribly articulate specialists, freed from classroom concerns, and let loose on a giant ego-trip. By the experts, for the experts, with little relevance when you attempt to translate their stimulating ideas into the classroom and integrate them with everything else you're trying to do.'[1]

With classroom reality clearly in mind, two basic guidelines can be recommended for the promotion of Designing and Making:

(a) it cannot be justifiably forced by unimaginative planning or rigid timetabling into a weekly 'slot'; and

(b) it must be set in a context that gives children the opportunity to involve themselves in real problem-solving.

This perspective reinforces the earlier claim that Designing and Making should not stand as a subject, but should be applied as an approach to learning – an approach that can in principle be integrated with most, if not all major aspects of the planned curriculum. In practice, however, projects and topics prove the most fertile and appropriate context for Designing and Making.

Why topics and projects?

Many teachers would offer the following types of comment in support of the general educational value of topics and projects:

— Topics and projects are a means of promoting more realistic and integrated learning experiences for children. They usually involve a direct, 'practical' base of experience for children set within a multi-disciplinary approach to an overall theme.

— The typically broad 'umbrella' themes for topics and projects readily encourage children to contribute their personal interests and insights to the development of themes. This motivational element considerably strengthens the impact of the work upon children's experience and learning.

In terms of Designing and Making, the topic and project setting offers four advantages:

1. The outline themes devised by the teacher usually offer a rich source of starting points for problem-solving through Designing and Making. Of equal importance, however, is the manner in which children's interest and contributions to those themes can readily expose starting points. As a result, the teacher is not continually faced with the need to contrive pre-set problems for Designing and Making. The children-teacher dialogue helps the teacher to avoid the dangers of teacher-imposition and contrivance – dangers that could effectively trivialise Designing and Making.

2. Topics and projects usually involve a strong element of individual and small-group activities. This small-group focus is particularly suited to Designing and Making. It creates a 'team setting' in which problem-solving can develop. A team not only provides a source of inspiration and feasible proposals. It can

also undertake real responsibility for the direction and quality of the Designing and Making. In this sense, individual responsibilities can evolve against a background of co-operation and mutual support.

The small-group base greatly facilitates the organisation and management of Designing and Making within a classroom. Under this system, teachers can easily organise Designing and Making as one of the several small-group activities that evolve during the topic or project. (Designing and Making is not restricted to one particular group for the duration of a topic. As the work progresses, new groups will form. Typically these groups will consist of a maximum of six to eight children at any one time.) This tactic shifts the focus of resourcing Designing and Making from the potentially overwhelming demands of an entire class to the much more modest and realisable requirements of a small group. Thus, the small-group organisation typical of topic and project work assists Designing and Making to become a realistic proposition for the classteacher.

3. The organisation of topics and projects is generally quite liberal and flexible in the use of time. This is particularly significant for Designing and Making since problem-solving activities do not readily lend themselves to strict, pre-set allocations of time. In contrast, they require time to be used by the teacher as

an 'adjustable' resource to support the continuity of the children's work. In this respect, topics and projects form a very appropriate setting for Designing and Making.

4. Topics and projects form part of the programmes of work devised by the majority of classteachers. Therefore, in terms of current practice, the curriculum setting for Designing and Making is already very familiar and well established. The promotion of Designing and Making does not require teachers to introduce a new subject into their schemes of work. What is sought is a subtle shift of emphasis in the nature of the children's experience[2] – a move towards a more child-centred approach, the development of problem-solving and the recognition of the educational value of practical activity. Hopefully, the fact that the introduction of Designing and Making is a matter of integration and consolidation of 'good' practice could contribute to its more widespread adoption by primary teachers.

Making A Start

If topics and projects form the appropriate setting for primary Designing and Making, how can a teacher actually 'start' Designing and Making? There are four preliminary points:

1. It would be wrong to assume that every topic and project should necessarily contain a Designing and Making element. In fact, when one reflects upon the range of planned curricular inputs relevant to topics or projects, one is faced with the obvious need for careful selection and management of inputs in the interests of a well-balanced programme for children throughout their primary years.

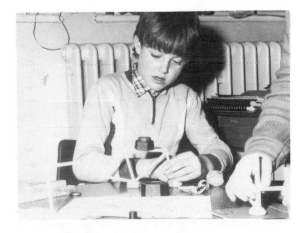

2. It is vital to view Designing and Making as a process of problem-solving – not craft! The experience for children of Designing and Making from the initial awareness of a need, through to the production of a refined solution is arguably more important than the product itself.

3. Real problem-solving cannot be conveniently packaged within work-cards or design briefs. Logically there needs to be a problem-context in which children recognise a need before problem-solving can proceed. Typically, work cards and design briefs lead to a highly simplistic and mechanical experience of problem-solving in which both the problem and the solution has been pre-determined.

4. It is important for the teacher to clarify her/his intentions underlying the introduction of Designing and Making. It is not sufficient to launch into this type of work in the hope of vague outcomes! This in turn implies that any planning decisions taken by the teacher must be based firmly upon a knowledge of the children concerned, and her/his general aims and objectives over the school year.

There seem to be three distinctive types of teacher-approach to initiating Designing and Making:

(a) The teacher plans in outline a topic or project. From her/his knowledge of the class and the particular topic theme, she/he devises a specific Designing and Making assignment for the topic. For instance, for the general topic of 'Transport', the teacher may decide to set as the assignment 'Design and make a model land vehicle that is powered by a rubber band.' Since the Designing and Making activity is based upon a clearly stated assignment, the teacher can thoroughly research and resource the activity. This feeling of being in control of the activity makes this approach very acceptable with teachers who are 'new' to Designing and Making.

Beneath this apparent convenience, organisation and control lies the danger of an over-prescriptive view of what problem(s) a given theme will present to children. This approach runs the risk of trivialising the experience of problem-solving for children since it tends to ignore the context for problem-solving and present a semi-formed solution. For this reason, this article includes little reference to topic or project themes and related

Designing and Making 'problems'.

(b)   As experience and confidence develop, teachers recognise the limited scope for children's problem-solving inherent in the previous approach. Similiarly, they appreciate more clearly the range and diversity of problems that topics and projects can generate. Therefore, when planning a topic they tend to forecast a number of problems that could be expected to emerge without narrow prescription or contrivance. This forecast offers a pool of probabilities that helps the teacher to prepare for a potential range of resourcing and organisation requirements. As the topic unfolds, she/he is then able to support a variety of Designing and Making proposals from the children.

For example, in a project on 'Shops', one predictable focus of interest might be the packaging of goods. Another focus of interest could be advertising and the promotion of products. During the topic, some children may elect to design and make carrier bags and cartons for products of their choice. Other children may decide to design and make promotional packaging and wrapping material, adverts or display 'gimmicks'. In this case, the teacher would be prepared for these and similiar choices as a result of her/his forcast.

This approach is clearly more sophisticated than the former. Its particular merit is that it encourages a more genuine and comprehensive experience of problem-solving for children.

(c)   The third approach is not so much a matter of planning as an attitude on the part of the teacher. In this case, the teacher may have certain preconceptions about the range of Designing and Making opportunities that a certain theme will present. However, she/he carefully avoids predetermining the nature and outcomes of any Designing and Making. It is a 'wait and see' situation where the teacher tries to capitalise upon the children's responses to the theme.

For instance, in a Maths project on 'Time', some children became very involved in practical 'timing' experiments. They decided to make their own timers for a specific purpose. The teacher did not set or contrive this problem, nor could she forecast that this particular need would arise. It was really a question of the teacher meeting the children's request.

Similarly, work in a school garden 'patch' led to some unsuspected Designing and Making. A Reception class had been planting seedlings. After a time, the plot looked decidedly disorganised and many seedlings were in danger of being trampled. Some of the children noticed this. They also pointed out that they were no longer sure of where the rows of seedlings were, or who had planted each row. They wanted some form of marker system. This need led very naturally to the children investigating the problem, and designing and making their own markers for use in the school garden.

The important feature of these three approaches is not simply their differences, but the progression they represent in a teacher's confidence and understanding. There seems little point in describing and recommending a theoretically ideal approach if it requires an unrealistic level of initial teacher confidence and experience. The preceding descriptions may act as route markers for teachers to work out their own tactics. The most influential factor in this process is not a teacher's 'technical' knowledge or expertise. It is a teacher's appreciation of what constitutes problem-solving, and her/his confidence and ability to encourage children in this type of experience.

This comment relates directly to the very common observation from primary teachers that, because they tend to lack a 'technical' background, they feel unable to help children in Designing and Making. In answer to this, I have consistently placed the teacher firmly in the role of managing learning through problem-solving. Teacher-success in Designing and Making does not depend upon technical expertise so much as upon those fundamental professional qualities that apply across the curriculum.

There is a certain amount of craft and technological experience that teachers will come to need to support Designing and Making. Obviously, a measure of teacher intervention and 'teaching' is required. But very often teachers over-estimate this particular requirement. For instance, many teachers express deep concern about teaching craft techniques. Provided the teacher is not trying to force upon primary children secondary techniques, tools and materials, then the craft element is far less demanding than one might initially assume.[3] The same observation holds true for technology since at primary level the focus is upon practical experience and using 'common sense' to make things work.[4] Certainly, experience shows that INSET courses can usually provide this 'technical' input with relative ease.

Many teachers also feel that Designing and Making can only be started after a foundation of thorough craft teaching and techniques has been established. Obviously, craft techniques do need some teaching input if children are to apply them effectively and safely. However, technique teaching is best provided when children appreciate the need for a particular technique. Therefore, in Designing and Making techniques tend to be taught as the need arises through the children's work – not in isolation. This needs' approach is highly realistic when one remembers that at any one point the teacher is concerned with a maximum of 6–8 designers and makers in a group setting.

Resources

Resources were mentioned vaguely during the description of possible approaches to initiating Designing and Making. As with 'craft teaching', the issue of 'resources' is extremely important but capable of producing a false impression of Designing and Making.

Teachers tend to assume that resources for Designing and Making must involve predominantly tools, craft materials and science or technology equipment. Similarly, they assume that these resources must be rather 'specialist' – at the very least, not usually found in primary school.

This impression is quite false. The commonly available range of primary resources like 'found' materials, basic tools and science equipment can support the vast majority of Designing and Making activities. But before giving any details of particular resources, certain more general comments need to be made.

There are two very important resourcing issues that tend to be overlooked and can subsequently hold back the development of Designing and Making throughout a school:

●Designing and Making requires a considerable range of reference-type resources to initiate and support investigation, research and planning. Whether at Reception or Upper Junior (Y6) level, children need appropriate resources to make informed decisions throughout their problem-solving. Therefore, specific provision must be made for this aspect of resources. A general outline of resources is presented in the Appendix

●As emphasised above, Designing and Making involves resource-based learning. Consequently, children must be able to access independently the vast majority of the relevant resources. This implies that the school's resources should be organised and managed with this need in mind. Resourcing for Designing and Making cannot be viewed simply as the development of a wide range of resources. It requires a school policy and system to facilitate 'open access' by children to resources not held within classrooms. It also calls for the creation of a highly portable or mobile resource facility that can be used conveniently within each classroom.

A mobile or portable storage system for basic tools, materials and equipment is vital if Designing and Making is to be accommodated efficiently within each classroom. Many schools base their facility around a light-weight, purpose-built carrying case or trolley. Trolleys have the additional advantage of extra carrying capacity for materials and equipment. In addition to mobility of basic constructional resources, trolleys and carrying cases ensure that resources can be organised, presented and cared for in a professional manner. This not only aids the efficient management of resources, but also has an influence upon children's attitudes to the work.

Some schools complement the trolley or carrying case system with a set of very light-weight drop-over tops that instantly convert a table or desk into an attractive activity-area for Designing and Making. As with the constructional resources, these tops can be easily moved from classroom to classroom.

Classroom Management and Organisation

It is a statement of the obvious but Designing and Making activities will often require thoughtful management and organisation of the classroom. Basically, the need for a specific organisation occurs when a Designing and Making group has progressed from initial research and planning to the point when it wants to construct prototypes of solutions and, subsequently, a finalised version of the solution.

At this point the group needs an area that will support a range of 'research and development' and constructional activities. For instance, children may want to construct with card, 'found' objects or wood. They may decide to set up Lego models to test out designs. They may need to experiment with, for example, lighting circuits. In other words, the group needs an activity-area that remains relatively undisturbed by the ebb and flow of classroom life.

One immediate answer might be to let the children work outside the classroom. Apart from general safety considerations, that tactic is educationally unsound. For instance, it segregates Designing and Making from the apparently mainstream classroom activities. It prevents other children in the class from sharing the experiences of a Designing and Making group. It makes sensitive teacher guidance extremely difficult. Finally, it may even discourage or prevent some teachers from attempting to involve Designing and Making in their schemes of work. Despite individual differences, teachers' solutions to this accommodation challenge share the following characteristics:

- The Designing and Making activity-area is set up in a part of the classroom that is outside the major thoroughfares used by children. (It would be unwise, however, to confine Designing and Making within a corner since a corner position can pose problems for long-range teacher supervision.)
- The activity-area is formed from ordinary classroom desks or tables – equipped ideally with drop-over tops.
- The area is kept clear of 'obstacles', eg sandwich boxes, sports bags, musical instrument cases, etc.
- There is a high level of natural and artificial lighting in the area.
- The area allows children easy access to resources, eg trolley or carrying case, craft materials or reference-type materials.
- It has display facilities that the children can use as an 'open' folder for the work under development. This feature – involving real, not exhibition work – can be particularly influential since it provides a direct means of sharing information and experience throughout the class.

When one considers the portable or mobile resource facility that underpins this approach, then the temporary re-organisation of a classroom proves very simple and convenient.

Conclusions

The review of classroom management and organisation marks a convenient 'breaking-off' point for this discussion. So what have I tried to achieve?

I set out to sketch in broad outline one model for a curricular starting point for primary Designing and Making, and raised some immediate, practical issues that influence any attempt to introduce Designing and Making. I have not looked much beyond the opening move of a Designing and Making initiative within a school. For instance, there has been insufficient space to explore issues of more long-term consequence such as:

- progression and continuity within Designing and Making, across the nursery-primary phase and onwards throughout the secondary phase.
- sex stereotyping and bias in Designing and Making.
- professional development needs of teachers in relation to Designing and Making.

I have, in particular, discouraged the packaging of Designing and Making in terms of topic or project themes and 'instant' Designing and Making assignments.

I have, however, presented, one very important and optimistic message: that Designing and Making is very much in sympathy with the aims and objectives of good primary practice, and can be highly relevant in the general education of primary children.

The implication in this message is that it is the particular responsibility of primary teachers, headteachers and advisers to ensure that Designing and Making is firmly and consistently rooted in 'good' primary practice. Undoubtedly, much of the spirit of Designing and Making already exists and flourishes in primary classrooms. The development of Designing and Making requires a sensitive extension and expansion of this 'good' practice. This is a pioneering challenge. Designing and Making offers an exciting dimension to the primary curriculum. We need the conviction and confidence to realise that potential.

References

[1] Sandford P. (1986), 'The hills were alive', TES. 4. 7.

[2] Williams P. H. M. (1985), *Teaching Craft Design and Technology 5–13*. Croom Helm.

[3] Williams P. and Jinks D. (1985), *Design and Technology 5–12*. (Ch 7). Falmer Press.

[4] DES (1985), *The Curriculum from 5–16*. HMSO para 87.

Appendix: Resources for Designing and Making

The following lists present an outline guide to the range of resources required for Designing and Making. No information has been given concerning recommended suppliers since LEAs usually have their own specific arrangements in this respect.

Reference-Type Resources

Books	Magazines	Leaflets	Brochures	
Posters	Pictures	Slides	Filmstrips	Videos

Cassettes/Recordings of Radio Programmes
Toys   Mechanical Artefacts
Constructional/Technology Kits, eg Lego, Capsela, Meccano, Fischer-technik

Natural and 'found' objects

Constructional Resources

'Found' Materials:

Matchboxes	Cardboard Boxes and Tubes	Plastic Bottles and Containers
Soft Drink Cans	'45' Records	Coffee-jar lids
Cardboard discs	Rubber Bands	String
Wire Coathangers	Wood Shavings and Sawdust	
Beads	Wool	Fabrics
PVC Tubing	Balloons	
(narrow diameter)		

Wood

Softwood off-cuts – planed all-round and in a variety of cross-sectional dimensions up to 25mm x 10mm. The most useful size is 10 x 10 mm.
Dowel, eg diameters 3mm and 4.5 mm
Balsa
Jelutong is an ideal wood for young children. It is worth buying one of the special 'primary' packs that a number of the major suppliers offer. These packs are particularly useful since their contents have been adjusted to suit the general requirements of primary Designing and Making.
For further information about wood, especially Jelutong, please contact your local CDT Adviser.

Plastics

For most activities, 'found' plastics materials will prove very suitable.

Metal

There is often a need for short strips of thin aluminium (18 or 20 gauge). For safety reasons, tinplate should not be used.

Card

The value of card as a constructional material is easily overlooked because it seems so 'ordinary'. It has, however, many advantages for young children. Therefore, it is worth developing stocks of different thickness, colour and quality of card.

Adhesives

PVA glue and Balsa Cement
Pritt

Fasteners

Sellotape   Masking Tape   Paper Clips   Paper Fasteners
Drawing Pins   Stapler   Blue-Tak
To a very limited extent, panel pins, screws, nuts, bolts and washers.

Finishes

The general range of 'finishes' used in Art and Craft activities will be very relevant for Designing and Making.

Tools

Safety Rules
Scissors and Craft Knives
Junior Hacksaws or Mini Hacksaws (with spare blades)
Hammers (Warrington 6oz)
Hand Drill and Twist Drill Set
Small Screwdriver (75 mm)
Electrical Screwdriver
Wire Stripper
Centre Punch
Hole Punch
Clamp-on Vices
Bench-hooks (primary sizes)
Drop-over Table or Desk Tops
Glasspaper (various grades)

Reminder: Tools housed in a carrying case or trolley.

'Technology' Resources

Technology/Constructional Kits – See reference-type resources for details.
Electrical Components – general primary science resources such as
                        insulated connecting wire; crocodile clips;
                        batteries; bulbs; bulb holders; switches;
                        electric motors; bells; buzzers.
Mechanical Components – wheels from broken toys; cardboard, plastic
                        or wooden discs; gear wheels and pulleys;
                        propellers; rubber bands.

PRIMARY SCHOOL TECHNOLOGY: where is it going?

Ann Smits   *Booth Wood Primary School, Loughborough*

Introduction

The intention of this article is to share some thoughts and experiences of primary school technology so that teachers may analyse their own ideas and practice. It is not to provide answers, for I believe those answers, ultimately, must come from primary teachers themselves when they have thought more deeply and had more experience of technology and related activities.

The encouragement of the development of technology in the primary school has led to confusion about what is expected and a feeling of inadequacy in many a conscientious teacher, who is, more often than not, female with a limited background in CDT or science. This has come about, I believe, because the term technology is linked to secondary school subjects (CDT) usually taught by a male teacher, specifically trained for the job, employing specialist knowledge, skills, tools and materials.

However, encouraged by the view of Tope (in *We can do it now,* an Equal Opportunities Commission publication[1]) that the main criterion for a teacher undertaking primary school technology 'is not his or her sex, but the enthusiasm for the subject, and enterprise in developing ideas which can lead to the use of technology', I set about introducing CDT into the school curriculum.

I attended a course made up of a series of meetings to discover the purpose and ethos behind primary technology and to learn a simple construction technique for use with young children. Subsequently, I organised an in-service workshop for teachers from local schools to which the teachers brought two pupils each and teachers and children worked side-by-side at acquiring the necessary skills to carry out constructions – in this case a simple chassis – which were tested and evaluated at the end of the day-long session.

The constructions were based on a technique pioneered by Jinks[2] and consisted of employing wood strip, dowel, card and adhesive for building structures to which a variety of materials and parts can be added to make models. The general philosophy behind this technique is that young children should be able to make accurate strong models safely, using simple, readily available tools and materials in the primary school classroom. Once the technique has been learnt it is hoped that it will be adapted by teachers and children according to the current topic, project or field of interest, whenever possible.

A survey of primary school technology

In the Summer term of 1986 I carried out a survey of primary schools in order to obtain information about the use to which the above construction technique was being put, teachers' attitudes to primary technology and their perceptions of future needs. An attempt was also made to define and identify the practice of primary technology. An 'opportunity' sample of 12 schools catering for the nursery/infant/junior age range was chosen from those schools who had put forward teachers to attend the above in-service course and other schools in which I had personal contacts. One might assume that such a sample would have a bias towards technology in the curriculum; on the other hand schools' participation in such courses might just as well indicate an interest in curriculum development in general.

Semi-structured, informal interviews were used, based on a questionnaire designed to elicit general information about the organisation of the curriculum of the school, values and attitudes towards primary school technology, availability and use of resources and current practice. In many cases I was able to speak to children in their classrooms also. In order to supplement the evidence collected in interviews, I also used informal observation. As in the case of the questionnaire, notes were made at the time and immediately after the visit, mainly about:

(a) displays and resources;
(b) the way in which teaching areas were used;
(c) the amount of pupil-initiated work;
(d) the opportunity available for the children to display individuality in their work.

I chose these aspects since I felt they would reflect the school ethos, the degree to which pupils are encouraged to speculate, evaluate and think for themselves and attitudes of the teachers towards these activities and technology.

Defining primary school technology

In order to identify the practice of technology in the primary school, I had to arrive at a definition of what I was seeking.

DES documents[3], reports from the Engineering Council and Standing Conference of Schools' Science and Technology[4] and Schools Council documents[5] all emphasise the extent of the interested bodies and the wide application of the term technology when applied to the primary school curriculum.

In 1980, when searching for a definition of CDT, HMIs highlighted the general acceptance of the fact that

'boys and . . . girls in school should discover the physical and aesthetic qualities of materials, acquire the skills to shape them and perhaps, above all, learn to plan and to execute work of their design'.[3]

Two years later the East Anglian Examination Board was quoted as defining technology thus:

'the identification of the needs of man and the endeavour to satisfy those needs by the application of science and use of materials, resources and energy. It is concerned with solving problems where there is no right or wrong answer . . . Technological behaviour requires activities that are creative and demanding . . . involves approaches and techniques . . . that are more than pure science or craft'.

Added to this was the view of CDT teachers that technology in school should include an active involvement on the part of pupils in making and designing artefacts or systems.[3]

Problem Solving: Science and Technology in Primary Schools[4] recognised five areas in the curriculum which contained activities that offer some links to the man-made world – primary science, primary craft, design and technology, mathematics, problem solving and the new technologies.

In the same year, 'designing and making' became the main title of an exhibition of CDT work from children of all ages and was adopted as a term more suited to primary school work 'which has as its particular focus the man-made world of objects and devices', and in which three levels of activity can be identified. 'The first level is that in which there is no three-dimensional construction and the child's designing is shown by drawing and writing . . . At this level the range of activities is confined to:
thinking,
speculative designing,
evaluating.
. . . The second level is that in which the results are shown by model making using soft materials, scrap materials and constructional kits. At this level a restricted range of activities occurs:
thinking,
speculative or practical designing,
constructing malleable or kit materials to make models of real objects,
evaluating.
. . . The third level is that in which the results are shown by an object or device that actually functions in some intended way made in any appropriate material, and capable of being evaluated in real terms. At this level a full range of activities occurs:
thinking,
practical designing,
constructing resistant materials to make a real object or device,
evaluating.' (quoted from Brough)[6]

In looking for instances of practice of primary school technology, the recognition of the three levels of activity above in conjunction with the five curriculum areas offering links to the man-made world was taken as a guide to evidence of such practice, and will suffice for this discussion although the combination of designing and making has wider implications for cross-curricular activity.

Due to the often brief and limited observations of ongoing and displayed work, usually gathered during a single visit to any one school, this section of the report will be confined to an overall view of activities in the schools surveyed in (1) the nursery/infant age range and (2) the junior age range.

1. *The nursery/infant age range*

Three different recurring science themes observed in the schools were 'sound', 'electricity' and 'magnetism'. Simple concepts concerning electricity and magnetism were shown to the children and they incorporated them into simple toys and games, using mostly scrap materials. Similarly, children were helped to make a variety of instruments to be plucked, hit or shaken. No formal designing or planning was observed, nor much evaluation, but children often decorated their instruments individually and talked to each other and their teachers about the activities.

In a topic on 'water' children were encouraged to design boats before making 'junk models' – few floated for long due mainly to unsuitable materials, gaps in construction, but the teacher seized on these opportunities to explore the properties of different materials, concepts of floating and sinking, weight and balance.

Within a topic about 'wind' infants made windmills; others made carts from boxes during an exploration of 'shape' – in both cases thinking and evaluating took place within the activity of making. 'Mirrors' was another starting point for model making in the infant classroom and the children made kaleidoscopes.

In one school the children had been introduced to levers, gears and pulleys through experience of lifting, pulling and turning. The teacher had made visual aids from cotton reels, card circles and had displayed cogs; a pulley was suspended from the classroom ceiling; children experimented with levers – a staple remover, a claw hammer, a see-saw, and they looked at mechanisms of clockwork toys. A visit to a local engineering workshop in which levers, cogs and pulleys were seen in action was another aspect of the topic. The children drew pictures and wrote about their experiences and observations. No designing or model making was noted but this was an ongoing topic and could well introduce these aspects at a later date.

'Bridges' was a topic in another infant classroom in which the teacher had consciously introduced all the aspects of designing and making. After a television programme, children had experimented with structures and spans and had been introduced, in a very simple way, to different sorts of bridges; they had made drawings of their favourite kind of bridge and had constructed models and tested them. There were fantastic models as well as 'sensible' ones and in true infant fashion the children were usually able to justify and explain the discrepancies between drawing and model.

One teacher arrived at the topic of 'bridges' by another route. The children started off by looking at plane shapes; they identified them in the environment and made them up out of kits, discarded materials, plasticene, etc. Through trial and error they discovered that the triangle provided strength to a construction and they built bridges and other structures.

In all these activities it was mainly through spoken language that the thinking, speculative designing and evaluating was carried out. Model making was often the start of the exercise or a way of applying simple scientific concepts. It is worth noting that most infant teachers had not considered that they were introducing technology to the children.

2. The junior age range

'Magnetism', 'electricity' and 'sound' were science topics which also occurred at least once in the junior school classes of the survey. Again, the principles learnt were incorporated into games, toys and instruments. Evidence of thinking, designing (guided and limited), constructing real objects (easier when applied to toys) and evaluating was noted.

In the case of the 'sound' topic, evaluation was carried out not only according to consideration of function (can you get a noise from it?) but also according to aesthetic considerations (does it sound pleasant? Is the shape and decoration attractive?).

'Bridges' were a centre of interest again, with television providing the initial stimulus, but the teacher concerned shelved the project until she could approach it better prepared, since she realised that the children's background knowledge was inadequate for what they were trying to do in their model making. The same teacher had also done work on the construction and testing of model 'cable cars'. The children had made a variety of models, without much prior thought, which they tested and evaluated as a group. They subsequently chose two of the ideas on which to base their final designs and set about drawing and making plans and models. Much work evolved around the exploration of angles, friction, and pulleys and the children recorded their ideas and evaluations through writing and drawing.

Within the aspect of primary craftwork came the making of 'puppets' stimulated by a language exercise which required the children to follow written instructions to construct their models. Each child went on to design individual dress and features for their puppets and they were planning to write a play and design a stage set.

Another junior class had had a brief introduction to the concept of 'shock absorption' and had touched on the relationship between weight, speed, force, impact, compression and had explored ways of presenting paper to absorb impact and minimise damage. The exercise involved the examination and evaluation of principles for future use rather than designing of an object to which to apply them. Discussion and written and drawn records encouraged thinking.

By far the most popular model making undertaken in eight classes within four schools was that of a basic 'chassis' which, in seven out of the eight classes, was based on Jinks' construction technique. In most cases, one of the main aims had been to introduce children to the simple technique and to the use of suitable tools. From this beginning many children went on to modify their chassis and to design and make superstructures after they had tested their models for smooth, straight running and had modified them accordingly. Some of the children were set tasks such as finding ways of getting the 'vehicles' to travel uphill or to stop at a given distance. One group of children decided they wanted their models to turn in a circle; they observed and discussed a Lego model produced by a member of the class and enlisted the help of an adult to modify original designs. Basic chassis work was quite prescriptive but many children put a lot of individual thought and work into finishing touches and shared their ideas.

A top junior class (Y6) converted their basic chassis into 'war machines' in an exploration of propulsion and trajectories and adapted the technique to make structures other than chassis. The children illustrated written accounts of their work and evaluated and modified their models.

In yet another school the teacher in charge of science started a topic by looking at ways of moving objects leading to the topic of 'wheels' which in turn led to the making of wheels of all sizes from a variety of card, wood and scrap materials and applying them to model vehicles. Concepts similar to those explored by the children above were introduced, drawing generally being carried out after the model making.

The five curriculum areas linked to primary school technology

In both infant and junior classrooms the activities observed contained evidence of primary science, craft, maths and problem solving – the new technologies area of the curriculum was not apparent.

Within the survey it was difficult to find an activity which involved all these areas. Typically, science predominated, yet in the infant school craft, design, technology and problem solving occurred during the development of manipulative skills, through insights gained into properties of materials, the improvisations and modifications made to drawings and models after simple

tests and evaluations, the assembling a components from a kit, the acquisition of simple technological language such as 'axle', 'bolts', 'pulley', 'power', etc. Maths was going on in the children's counting, ordering, matching, measuring, comparing, exploring of two and three dimensional shapes, open and closed spaces – all part of their drawings and/or model making.

The making, testing and modifying of vehicles in some junior classes also branched out from craft work into problem solving and science, and embracing some maths and elements of art.

The three levels of designing and making

The first level frequently occurred within the younger age range of the school and the second level often overlapped the first. In the infant classroom, the distinctions between thinking, designing, evaluating and model making were blurred. The child would talk about the picture he had drawn of his pedal-car, explaining how he thought it worked, justifying the inclusion of that wheel or this light, perhaps modifying his picture as new ideas or discrepancies occurred to him through his communication with a peer or the teacher. Children were observed talking to themselves as they put their ideas down on paper, correcting themselves verbally and through their drawings. The child also used his model making in the same way – whether made from discarded materials or commercially produced kits such as Lego, Bigbuilder, Educastor, etc. Occasionally, children would draw and make models.

The first two levels are obviously an important preparation for the third and it is feasible to assume that those children who had gone through the stages of speculative designing and model making would be ready to design in a practical way and possibly make a real object or device; however, not many of the older children were thinking and designing before making models and evaluating was not always carried out; few children experienced success at the third level. The synthesising effect of design, observed in infant activities and which David Jinks and Pat Williams[2] consider to be one of its most valuable contributions to the curriculum, was lost.

Is it primary school technology?

In considering whether the activities observed in the schools can be termed primary school technology it is useful to refer to some of the definitions referred to earlier in this article:

> Children 'should, above all, *learn to plan and to execute work of their own design*'.

'Technological behaviour requires activities that are *creative and demanding*' and 'involves approaches and techniques that are *more than pure science or craft*'. (DES)[6]

From the survey it would appear that the elements of individual designing and planning and the intellectually demanding and creative aspects of the children's work are the weakest points of their technological activities – the bulk of the work being reliant on the science and craft areas of the curriculum.

Confusion and inadequacy

In these circumstances it is surprising, therefore, to record some of the respondents' views of the special contribution that primary school technology has to make to the curriculum:– the importance of the cognitive aspects of thinking, planning and evaluating was mentioned as well as the way in which understanding is promoted through the recognition of relevance rather than the mere acceptance of facts; the development of personal qualities such as perseverance and self-sufficiency and the synthesising effect of design-related activities right across the curriculum were also introduced as positive benefits to be gained from primary school technology.

So why are these aspects under-represented in the primary school classroom? One reason may be the confusion that surrounds the definition of primary school technology; some respondents identified it as 'up-to-date craft work', the 'physics of science', 'applied science', 'it must have wheels – it's to do with things that move', 'it's making models' . . . 'problem solving' . . . 'acquainting children with industry'.

Another contributory factor is the fact that all but one of the teachers interviewed were women, most of whom were ready to believe that they were 'not very good at technology' yet were delighted to discover that they could, in fact, use tools and design and make things when they attended courses.

Flood[7], adviser to the DES film 'Technology Starts Here' and Central Television's 'Starting Science', believes that in primary school technology a 'controlled, prescriptive phase is necessary to ensure that children get some initial success and begin to characterise themselves a "good at this". He goes on to say that the justification of this phase is when 'it leads to a second phase where both [teacher] and pupils have a rich opportunity to explore further problems and possibilities on a more individual basis'.

Just as children need guidance in thinking, designing, making and evaluating, so do many teachers need to have a 'prescriptive phase' to launch them successfully into a way of teaching that may be new to them.

Science schemes and primary school technology

Another set of responses worth examining in more detail is that concerned with the curriculum areas thought to be most closely involved with primary school technology.

Half the interviews were conducted with the teacher interested in science, two with the art and design specialists and the remainder with a head teacher or teacher with no main interest.

One can assume that many of the responses to the questionnaire and activities selected for observation would be based on the viewpoint of a person particularly interested in science. Science was put forward as having the strongest link with technology (9/10 schools) and craft was mentioned as being important from the model making and decorative aspect (8/10 schools). From the summary of activities observed in the primary school it can be seen that science topics provide most of the stimuli.

With this in mind, four primary science schemes were briefly examined for technological content employing the criteria discussed in the definition used for this survey:

Science 5–13. (Schools Council), 1973 MacDonald Educational.[3]
Learning through Science. MacDonald Educational.[3]
Science Horizons. (West Sussex 5–14 Scheme).[8]
Exploring Science and Technology. 1986, C.U.P.[9]

In all these schemes the elements of speculative and practical designing and the construction of models and real objects or devices was very limited. Despite a good deal of background material which could provide a basis for 'designing and making', the designs were given and instead of evaluation and modification the children were asked to observe and record.

Many questions asked of the children on workcards suggested a closed 'yes' or 'no' answer; eg 'Can you . . .?' not 'How can you . . .?' The most recently published scheme, 'Exploring', has a 'more to explore' card for each of its 12 modules which introduce more technological content – some design is mentioned (ie drawing and planning) but not emphasised. The authors, despite the title of the scheme, have not paid much attention to children's needs to 'learn to plan and execute work of their own design', or the importance of encouraging 'activities that are creative and demanding' and 'approaches and techniques that are more than pure science or craft'.

The importance of drawing within the design activity

Children's growing awareness of the elements of art (line, pattern, shape, colour, texture, etc), the use children make of their drawings, particularly the younger ones, in clarifying and expanding their ideas and the emphasis placed on planning and designing by Brough (1985) reflect the concern of HMI that 'boys . . . and girls in school should discover the physical and aesthetic qualities of materials'. DES (1980). Unfortunately, the survey demonstrated that many children were less inclined to use drawing as they progressed through the primary school.

John Steers[10], General Secretary of the National Society for Education in Art and Design, regrets the exclusion of the word 'art' from design policy documents.

> 'Teaching "awareness" of design and its process is not enough. One of the essential areas they (teachers) must teach is intelligent observation and analytical freehand drawing . . . Drawings are often a surer guide to a designer's thinking, and the quality of that thinking, than verbal analysis'.

It is interesting to note here the comments received from four CDT departments in secondary schools that receive most of the children from the schools involved in the survey. Although their organisations and programmes of work differed a great deal, all stated that they would like children to have done more drawing in their primary schools – both from observation and as a means of planning and designing work.

Also, it was thought that most children, at the age of 11, still tended to regard a piece of work as 'a one-off' and they were not accustomed to persevering with their work, to evaluating it and modifying it.

In conclusion

Several areas in the primary school curriculum were identified in which work of a technological nature was being done, the area of science predominating; but the important aspect of evaluation was not being fully exploited and the weakest elements were those of planning and designing.

The strong bias towards science appears to be at the neglect of other areas. However, this relationship with science may be necessary if technology is going to be taken seriously in the primary school, because science is beginning to acquire the status of a 'basic' in the curriculum, along with mathematics and language. This implies that the subject is indispensable to a child's education and is self-perpetuating since schemes of work, methods of evaluating and recording, etc, appear in the schools, in-service courses are set up, all of which are seen as a justification for developing the subject and giving it more curriculum time. It also helps to reduce the confusion and feelings of inadequacy which were made so apparent through this survey.

However, in the long-term, this alliance with science may distort primary school technology since its application may be restricted to scientific knowledge and procedures and prevent the child from using common sense, everyday knowledge, gained from a *variety* of experiences, in the solution of problems.

In conjunction with designing, technology has an important part to play in providing a link between the cognitive and practical aspects of learning, in pulling together the threads of the curriculum and introducing relevance into children's schooling. For this reason alone it should not be seen to be tied too strongly to any one curriculum area.

Finally, I return to the purpose of this article, which is to encourage those in primary education to think more deeply about their practice, for, as in all areas of the curriculum the success or failure of any initiative and the quality of the child's learning experience rests on the understanding, commitment and expertise of the teacher.

References

1. Everley, B. (1982) *We Can Do It Now!* EOC.
2. Jinks, D. and Williams, P. (1985) *Design Technology 5–12.* Falmer Press.
3. DES (1980) *Craft, Design and Technology in Schools: Some Successful Examples.* HMSO, and; DES (1982) *Technology in Schools: Developments in Craft, Design and Technology Departments.* HMSO.
4. The Engineering Council, SCSST. (1985) *Problem Solving: Science and Technology in Primary Schools.*
5. Schools Council (1973) *5–13 Project Nuffield Junior Science.* MacDonald Educational, and; Schools Council (1984) *Learning Through Science.* MacDonald Educational.
6. Brough, L. (1985) *Designing and Making:*

Learning Through Craft, Design and Technology. East Midlands and Yorks Forum of Advisers in CDT.

7   Flood, J. (1983) *'Making Working Models Work'. In Primary Contact.*

8   West Sussex. (1985) *Science 5–14 Science*

Horizons. Macmillan Educational.

9   Cambridge University Press (1986) *Exploring Primary Science and Technology.*

10   Steers, J. (1986) *'The Hi-Jacking of Design'. Times Educational Supplement, 7.3.86.*

NURSERY CHILDREN AS DESIGNERS AND MAKERS

Caroline Matusiak *nursery teacher, Braeburn Infant School, Scarborough*

How can we ensure that process rather than product determines our use of scrap materials in the classroom?

All classrooms have junk modelling incorporated into their programme. Is it always the children who design their own models? Too often teachers decide that children are unable to make a worthwhile model, so the teacher stipulates which materials are to be used and how they are to be assembled. All the potential for problem solving and personal initiative is lost, as the child's contribution is reduced to little more than manipulative skills.

Only through exploration and experimentation can children learn about the properties of materials and acquire building skills. When children are familiar with resources, they begin to formulate their own ideas, testing different materials and methods in order to achieve their goal.

Setting up

In my nursery for 3-5 years, I have an area shelved at child height (Fig. 3.6.1). The shelves hold baskets (in our case plastic mushroom boxes from the market) containing all the materials for use. There is a large table for the children to work on, within easy reach of the paint should it be required. In addition, two large boxes hold a stock of cereal packets and other large containers. Natural and man-made materials are sorted into broad categories according to form. Materials include shells, cones, seeds, twigs, foil cases, bottle tops and cardboard. Anything goes!

No strict definition is possible as some articles fit two or more categories. However, the categories do serve a useful purpose in grouping materials of a similar form, so that should a child require an axle, there are several alternatives at hand to encourage thoughtful choice. Children participate in the sorting and consequent discussion, alerting themselves to the materials' potential (Fig. 3.6.2).

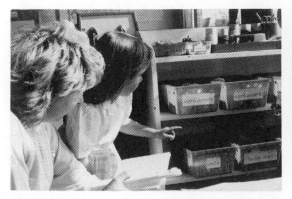

Figure 3.6.1

Figure 3.6.2

Children are more willing to search through a box if it is not too full, and they can sift easily through without spilling its contents. Their parents are encouraged to keep a bag by the kitchen bin in which to collect items for use in the nursery. We specialise in attic clearances!

In a tray with dividers, there are scissors, brass paper fasteners, paper clips, rubber bands, Blu-tak, string, wool and a stapler. PVA glue and paste are also provided.

Mark-making equipment is important as pencils and crayons are used to draw on models: figures seated in vehicles, a cross to distinguish an ambulance, or wavy lines for the sea. Children enjoy writing their own captions for display (often early mark-making) and are encouraged to write their 'name'. If required, the teacher will act as scribe writing down children's comments about their work. Older children draw plans of their work; model and plan are subsequently displayed together.

Display of models is welcomed by children and parents. It need not be a fixed display. My tables change daily because many children wish to take work home, others are happy for it to remain, while some show no further interest as the **doing** rather than the making is important.

Process not product

Thus access to a wide range of materials gives children opportunity to explore, handle and name a variety of shapes, sizes and textures. In the early stages there may be no attempt to bind together. Children discover what materials can and cannot do as they try to cut, bend, tear and fasten (Fig. 3.6.3). Skills such as fixing, folding and balancing develop simultaneously.

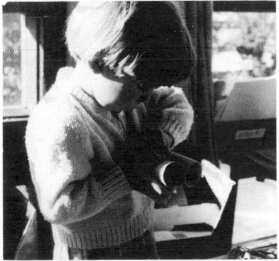

Figure 3.6.3

Through practical activity children gain experience of concepts such as vertical (piles of boxes), horizontal (rows of yoghurt pots) and 1 to 1 correspondence (one polystyrene chip to each division of an egg box). Children may explore a certain shape and its attachment to another surface. They may well sort similar objects or objects with similar properties as work becomes more thoughtful. These concepts are the basis of later maths, science and CDT.

Children engaged in self-directed activity do not always make something specific, for example, a boat. They may well make:

a. A construction that does something, 'This can open up.'

b. A construction that has certain attributes, 'This one has orange paper and seeds.'

c. A nameless construction, similar to one made with bricks, as a child develops skills of balance, 'Look how high it is.'

d. Patterns, sometimes symmetrical, 'It goes round and round.'

Children become aware of their ability to control and determine the making. Many children add an item through personal volition. 'There's grass on the roof because I want it.' Children are making choices about which materials to select and how to use them (Fig. 3.6.4).

Figure 3.6.4

Problem solving

Self-directed activity in the scrap materials area offers scope in problem solving for nursery children. Attaching materials offers a particular challenge. Children may experiment with the same binding on different materials, or with different bindings on the same material. Sophie (3 years 9 months) wanted to put a chimney on her building. She tried a roll but it fell; searching again in the materials, she emerged with a tooth-paste box which she glued on. 'There! I've done it. It sticks. It's got a lid under it.'

Models which do not work according to plan are just as interesting for discussion, analysis and consideration of future alternatives, as are 'successes'. A child needs time, space, materials and opportunity to experiment and discover without fear of failure.

Models may be repeated, either in an attempt to reproduce exactly, or to develop them with minor alterations; improving or expanding on the previous one. This repetition is similar to the way in which children build and develop their constructions in the Block Area.

Models can be tested. Russell (4 years 2 months) made two boats that were tested in the water tray, with the result that one sank and the other floated. Speculation about which boat might sink, why it sank, and how we could render it seaworthy, provided a wealth of discussion. Other children were motivated to make a boat and test it.

Challenges can be offered to more proficient model-makers, for example, to make something that floats or moves. Place is needed in the nursery to store unfinished models to which children may return.

Children bring their work to small group discussion, explaining how they were made, what they used, problems encountered and their solution. In this way, they share their knowledge and experience of materials in a useful way (Fig. 3.6.5).

Figure 3.6.5

Representation

A teacher can only determine when a child is representing, by talking with the child about the model or scene. As making proceeds, the model may be several different things. Gradually, models or scenes become more coherent. Hannah (3 years 8 months) made a sea, with engines, a fishing-line and 'things what the man can stand on to walk in the sea'. This representation was not readily identifiable by an adult, as a feather was a 'leaf' and the dried leaves were 'engines'. Finished products are rarely obvious to an adult at this early stage. A smear of glue and a scattering of sawdust

may have been a vital part of a child's storying in the Scrap Materials Area (Fig. 3.6.6). At an advanced stage, children will make totally imaginary represent-ations. Paul (4 years 9 months) made an 'Iki Tiki Poki and it goes anywhere'. He was consistent and coherent in naming parts and their functions.

To a child who is not yet able to represent, a teacher-directed model, for example a boat, is still simply, 'boxes'; and even those able to represent may well see something else, 'a house...and that is the chimney' or stare in disbelief at the pile of boxes the teacher insists is a boat. Told often enough that it is a boat, children will, of course, repeat it, but they still may not see it for themselves. Indeed, teacher-directed models may well inhibit the development of representation, as the child gets the message that only adult perception is valid.

Teacher role

Although the teacher is no longer directing and determining the outcome of the children's activity with scrap materials, she still has a vital role:

a. To sustain the child's concentration and effort with her interest.
b. To give language to the child's actions, providing words that a child can use later, 'I see that you are folding the paper'.
c. To encourage children to discuss what they are doing.
d. To encourage the development of ideas.
e. To be aware of the child's attempt to represent.
f. To challenge each child at his own level.
g. To respect whatever the child has been working on.

Figure 3.6.6
Sticky mess?

'Not another sticky mess!' are words from a parent that can destroy a child's confidence. On setting up the Scrap Materials Area, my first aim was to inform parents about what the children were learning. To this end, I set up a display board with a web of the language, maths, science and creative possibilities. Information sheets were sent home explaining that children were not shown how to make models. However, the importance of parents listening carefully to what children say about their work was emphasised (Fig. 3.6.7).

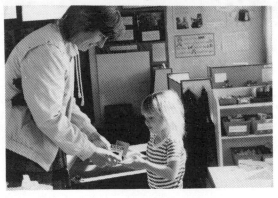

Figure 3.6.7

When parents arrive to collect children, I try to discuss what the child has done and how this was achieved. This is especially important with younger children who can readily identify their work, but are not always able to discuss it afterwards.

Parents are encouraged to work alongside their child. When Rickie (3 years 10 months) was making a collage of a man, his mum was there helping; pressing down the cheesebox 'face', holding wool for him to cut, and then while flicking off the extra sawdust 'hair', she discovered that non had stuck:

Mum: What did we forget?
Rickie: Glue!
Mum: Let's try again.

Later, on picking up the collage, Rickie found that the 'arms' (baby milk measures) fell off.

Mum: Will the arms be all right? Or could we use something else?

Rickie searched and glued again.

Rickie: There!

Mum: Straws this time. Not so heavy. They won't fall off.

When parents have watched their children making, they can appreciate the problem solving, effort and concentration that work requires. Now parents' greetings are far more encouraging, including, 'You have been busy!' and 'Tell me about it', which opens the way to a worthwhile discussion.

Parental support brings the encouragement a child needs to persevere in the mastery of materials. As teachers, we need to provide an area resourced with a variety of natural and man-made materials where children can make plans and try out different ideas. In making choices about what materials to use and how to use them, children develop initiative, independence and imagination. There is a sense of personal challenge that brings the satisfaction of achievement (Fig. 3.6.8).

Figure 3.6.8

DESIGN AND TECHNOLOGY:
early years and special educational needs

Clare Benson *advisory teacher for science and technology, Wolverhampton LEA*

The creation of the 'new' curricular area, 'Design and Technology', has brought feelings both of fear, insecurity and inadequacy and of anticipation, enthusiasm and excitement. Yet, as teachers, especially of Early Years and Special Educational Needs children, become familiar with the process of, and approaches to, Design and Technology, so they come to appreciate the area's value in helping these children to think for themselves, to co-operate and to work with others. Through Design and Technology, children are learning to face up to, and overcome, problems from a variety of situations both imaginary and real.

As with other 'new' areas, the dispelling of worries over content and application is all important and is often combined with the realisation that we are doing that already. By taking the five questions WHAT?, WHY?, WHO?, WHEN? and HOW?, and using them as a framework for a more detailed study of the implications of Design and Technology for Early Years and Special Educational Needs children, I hope to allay many previously held fears and to extend and develop certain already established ideas and approaches.

WHAT?

The technological process

Ask a group of Early Years or Special Educational Needs teachers to think of words that they associate with Design and Technology, and the list might include:

computers	Technic Lego	model making
machines	moving parts	problem solving
design	testing	micro-electronics

Design and Technology incorporates all these but is broader still; it must be viewed as an holistic process in which children are involved, and which, set in a variety of contexts, gives breadth and balance to their experiences. Recently, Design and Technology has tended to be linked to Science, especially for younger children, and teachers have felt that it is almost impossible to separate the two. Yet, it is clear now that Design and Technology could provide a starting point in its own right, drawing upon knowledge and skills both from Science and from other curricular areas. Although children studying Design and Technology will gain knowledge about Energy, Mechanisms and Structures, in the first instance the emphasis will be on the acquisition of knowledge about the properties and uses of materials. The latter should be acquired through a variety of contexts which include school, home, recreation, community, business and industry. Activities should be relevant and could arise from, for example a real life situation, play or a classroom topic. Although there are many situations that could be used, it is important that the approach that is adopted is not prescriptive as children should be able to make their own choices and decisions when working on a problem.

What then is this holistic process that children should experience?

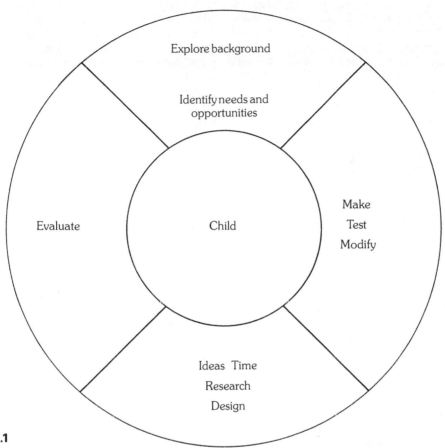

Figure 3.7.1

The child is at the centre of the process and although each area should be included, it will not necessarily be experienced in a linear way but in a process whereby each area will be visited and revisited during the course of the activity (Fig. 3.7.1). Particular consideration should be given to children with Special Educational Needs. It is a statutory requirement that maximum participation in Design and Technology activities is an entitlement for all, but some modifications will obviously be necessary depending on the physical, behavioural and mental abilities of the individual child. It would not make sense to disapply certain processes for whole groups of children, and therefore teachers must make their own decisions about disapplication for each individual child.

Having involved the children in the technological process, it will be possible for each child to work at his/her own level, thereby allowing the teacher to assess individuals while they participate in a group situation. It is vital that the process is seen as a whole and assessed accordingly. Indeed this may seem perfectly natural for teachers of Early Years children who are already involved in cross-curricular activities.

WHY?

The simple answer to this question would be that Design and Technology is now a compulsory subject, but it would be a sad reflection of education today if that is the only reason for its inclusion. So many of the skills and attitudes that are developed in Design and Technology are cross-curricular and through it pupils can gain a valuable understanding of a variety of issues concerned, for example, with environmental and social awareness, with business and economics and with health and safety. The capabilities of young children are continually underestimated and it is especially important that very young children are given the opportunity to develop the skills of communication and independent thought and the attitudes of co-operation and perseverance.

It is equally important to give children with Special Educational Needs opportunities that are similar to those of other children. Warnock maintains that the purpose of education is the same for all children and that there are two goals towards which they should be working, albeit at varying rates of progress; 'first, to enlarge a child's knowledge, experience and imaginative understanding; second, to enable him or her to enter the world after formal education is over as an active participant in society and a responsible contributor to it.' Design and Technology affords children the opportunity to travel towards these goals at their own speed.

WHO?

While the National Curriculum states that all core and foundation subjects, including Design and Technology, are an entitlement for every child aged five to sixteen, Early Years teachers would certainly argue that three and four year olds should be, (as indeed they already are), involved in Design and Technology activities. Moreover, teachers of children with Special Educational Needs will welcome their inclusion within the provisions of the National Curriculum. Indeed the Warnock report, while recognising the importance of social training, emphasises the fact that, 'a good educational programme is therapeutic and important to personal development.'

Although it is essential for these two groups of children to be involved, it is important to recognise some of the difficulties that may arise while trying to provide them with a broad and balanced curriculum. For example, it would be unacceptable to use programmes of study with three or four year olds with the idea of trying to 'push them up the ladder' of Statements of Attainment. However, by involving the children in a variety of tasks based broadly on the programmes of study, skills and attitudes will be fostered that can be built upon at a later stage.

For children with Special Educational Needs, the Design and Technology 5-16 proposals have highlighted two main aspects, those of 'Communication' and 'Making', both of which will present particular problems. 'Communication' in both oral and written form is a vital part of Design and Technology as it 'tells others about intentions, progress and problems as well as for clarifying and reconstructing ideas.' Therefore alternative ways of communicating must be used by those children who are unable to use the former, conventional methods. Body language and the computer are two very different, but very effective, ways that can

be used as a substitute for conventional communication.

Although 'Making' may prove impossible for some children, it is quite possible for a teacher or for peers to help with construction, following the ideas and instructions given to them. One such pupil, John, was able to 'make' very successfully a wheeled vehicle, although he could not talk or use his hands to hold materials and tools. By watching other children use different materials, fixings and mechanisms, he built up his own knowledge and when given a variety of choices at each stage of the construction of his model, he was well able to indicate his preference by the use of eye communication.

WHEN?

Officially, from September 1989, children aged 5-16 should have Design and Technology included in their curriculum for 'a reasonable amount of time'. Then, from September 1990, all children in Key Stage One will have to follow the Programmes of Study and the Attainment Targets laid down in the National Curriculum, with the first unreported assessment in Summer 1992. Children with Special Educational Needs will be required to follow the National Curriculum a year later. However, many children are already engaged in innovative programmes of work, covering much that has been outlined in the document and it would seem sensible to incorporate Design and Technology into curriculum planning as soon as possible.

While consideration should be given to the amount of time to be spent on Technological activities, it is almost impossible to separate individual subjects due to their cross-curricular nature. It is also important that a high degree of flexibility is built into the timetable. During the various stages of planning and designing, making and modifying, retesting and evaluating, children will work at different speeds; nothing is more frustrating than continually having to stop and restart a task and this should be taken into account when planning the outline of the day's programme.

HOW?

Getting started

Although many teachers lack confidence in their abilities and feel that they do little if any Technology, much work of this kind is already going on in many Early Years classrooms. It is important not to feel that all that has gone before is invalid but rather to try to build constructively upon these experiences. Often a change of emphasis is all that is necessary; encouraging children to explore and identify their own needs can change a prescriptive 'making and modifying' activity into one that involves the whole Technological process.

It is possible to separate the opportunities for developing activities into two categories - those that arise spontaneously from everyday situations and those that are introduced in a more structured way from, for example, through a classroom Topic. Both are valuable in different ways; while the former takes advantage of the immediate and relevant opportunities identified by the child, it may not provide sufficient variety of contexts within which the child can work to extend his/her knowledge and skills. It is often these kinds of activities in which both Early Years children and those with Special Educational Needs become engaged as they are best able to cope with concrete situations (arising from something with which they are immediately involved). It is therefore necessary to plan a balanced programme of work in order to ensure that the child is given the opportunity to experience a variety of contexts within which to develop his/her knowledge and skills.

Possible items from which spontaneous activities might arise

1   Sand tray — Building structures such as bridges, tunnels, castles and moats; Investigating and using materials such as wet and dry sand.
2   Water tray — Developing knowledge related to Energy through boats, fountains, water wheels etc.
3   Construction kit — Building structures such as towers, and climbing frames; Developing knowledge related to Energy and Mechanisms when, for example making vehicles move.
4   Home Corner — Designing the best arrangement for the area.
5   Shop — Investigating, designing and making packaging, shelving and items to sell.
6   Shelter — Designing and making a den. (both internal and external).
7   Games — Designing and making board games.
8   Playground — Devising a system for avoiding

'traffic congestion' when all the bikes are in use; Efficient usage of the area for different purposes.
9   Items from home — Investigating, designing and making toys, holiday ornaments etc.

Possible topics from which activities can be developed

As always, when choosing a Topic, it is important to ensure that it will be relevant to the child and will provide sufficient breadth from which to develop more than one or two areas of the curriculum.

The following is obviously not an exhaustive list but is intended as a starting point from which teachers can develop their own ideas.:

Ourselves	The playground
My family	Toys
My home	Out and about
Our classroom	Games
Our school	Water
Stories	The Park
Movement	Growth

The following examples indicate possible needs and opportunities that the children might identify from such Topics:

Our school
Raising money for the School Fund
Publicising an event such as Sports Day
Organising a celebration such as a Christmas party
Developing a piece of waste ground
Stories
Hansel and Gretel
A trail through the woods; something to help Hansel reach the key; something to help Hansel and Gretel cross the lake.
Three Pigs
An overnight bag; a strong straw or twig house; an alarm to announce the arrival of visitors.
The Park
Access to play equipment for the disabled; secure litter bins; a litter 'picker-up'; interesting play equipment; the design of land use.

Further discussion with the children may result in a planning sheet, similar to the one below (Fig. 3.7.2):

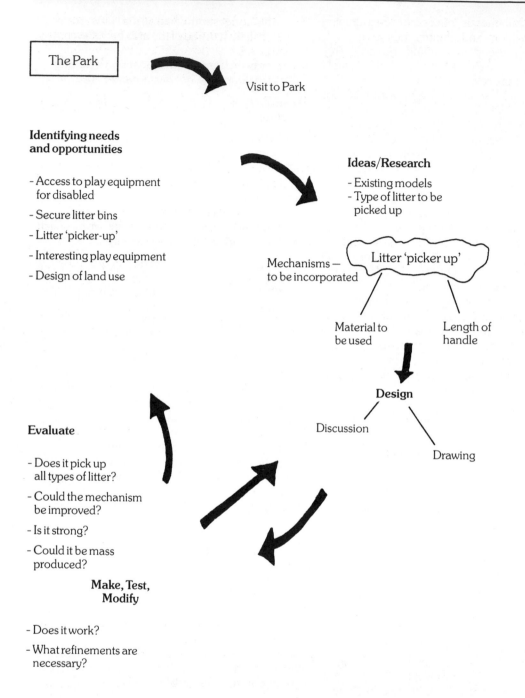

The Park

Visit to Park

Identifying needs and opportunities

- Access to play equipment for disabled
- Secure litter bins
- Litter 'picker-up'
- Interesting play equipment
- Design of land use

Ideas/Research

- Existing models
- Type of litter to be picked up

Mechanisms — to be incorporated

Litter 'picker up'

Material to be used

Length of handle

Design

Discussion

Drawing

Evaluate

- Does it pick up all types of litter?
- Could the mechanism be improved?
- Is it strong?
- Could it be mass produced?

Make, Test, Modify

- Does it work?
- What refinements are necessary?

Figure 3.7.2

How much time should be allocated?

Due to the cross-curricular nature of Design and Technology, it is almost impossible to prescribe in any precise way the exact amount of time involved. The National Curriculum suggests that activities should vary in length; and that depending on their scope, children should be involved in one or two in a term (with eight during Key Stage One). Of course, neither younger children nor those with Special Educational Needs may be able to persevere with an extended activity and a series of shorter tasks may therefore be more appropriate.

How to organise the classroom?

After children have been given time to settle in to a new environment, their first task could be to help design and organise the layout of the classroom (Fig. 3.7.3). (It is sometimes difficult, even for the most thoughtful adult, to be able to put him or herself in the place of a disabled or very small child.)

ways might be found to help children to work confidently by themselves or with their peers (thus enabling the teacher to give attention to individuals or a small group).

The following suggestions may prove helpful:

1   Ensure that the children are familiar with the whereabouts of resources and materials within the classroom.
2   Ensure that they know of any equipment that they are not allowed to use unsupervised.
3   Ensure that a high status is attached to such activities as working with jigsaws and construction kits, playing imaginatively and looking at, and reading books.
4   Ensure that all the children know that their turn for the teacher's assistance will come.
5   Encourage children to help, and work with, each other, rather than to always ask for adult help.
6   Encourage the idea that while the teacher is working with a group, the other children should try not to interrupt, but solve their own

Identified need - Efficient layout of classroom

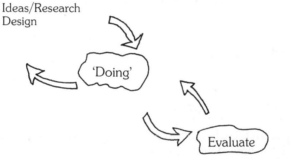

Ideas/Research
Design

'Doing'

Evaluate

Are items easily available?

Does the room look welcoming?

Are there areas for different types of activities?

Figure 3.7.3

The children gain much for taking responsibility from an early age for the real task; they are developing their skills of exploration, investigation, design, communication and appraisal; they are learning to co-operate and to listen to each other's ideas; they are gaining practical knowledge about the safe storage of tools and equipment; and they are building up an understanding of a system as well as developing their aesthetic awareness.

How to organise the activities

A common difficulty met by teachers of young children and of those with Special Educational Needs is the inability of the children to work independently, so that problems arise when supervision of a small group is necessary. Various

problems.

7   Use other adult help within the classroom wherever possible.

How to work

Grouping the children will vary with different activities but there are several issues that need to be considered. Young children are very pre-occupied with themselves and as a consequence often find it hard to work with more than one or two other children. It is necessary though to encourage a sharing both of ideas, and of practical help, from an early age so that it becomes part of the way of working. Other children, by the nature of their disability, may find difficulties in communicating with others or in offering physical help, but they should still be included in a group. They will learn much by watching or listening, while others in the group will learn to offer help at appropriate times.

Grouping should be varied to allow for friendship, and to create mixed ability or similar ability groups as required. Young children may find it less threatening to work with friends but by gradually varying the composition of the groups, children will gain confidence in working with other class members. One problem that is often raised is that of the dominant or very quiet child's position in a group. It is an important part of the learning process that we listen to each other — indeed many adults have not acquired this attitude — and the teacher should encourage a dominant child to realise the importance of this. One possible way of encouraging a child to become more vocal in a group situation is to ensure that he or she has taken part in something which is of particular interest. Of course, groups are not the only way to organise a class and at times, children may work as individuals, in pairs or even as a large group or as a whole class. It can be useful to identify needs and opportunities through a larger group discussion and for the children then to decide which avenues they wish to explore further.

How to organise equipment and resources

There is rarely adequate space for storage in a school and therefore a system could be established whereby some items are stored centrally, while others remain in the classroom. Young children quickly learn the whereabouts of different resources and it is important as part of their development that they can collect, from different sources, the items that they need (See Appendix).

As construction kits are very valuable for Technology, these should be distributed fairly throughout the school. Different kits have different strengths and weaknesses; some can be used relatively easily by children with physical disabilities while others require children to have a high degree of manual dexterity; while others can be used to develop specific areas of knowledge such as Mechanisms or Structures. Clearly it would be useful to compile a list of kits within the school along with a short description of their particular strengths and weaknesses.

How to communicate the children's findings

Writing is certainly not the only form through which children can communicate their findings. Indeed for those children, who for whatever reason, cannot write, alternative ways must be found (Fig. 3.7.4).

One further method might be for the teacher to keep a diary for each member of the class in which is recorded any particularly perceptive or enterprising observation or action. It is not intended that this should be a time consuming task but it would provide firm evidence of any progress made at the end of a project. Some children with Special Educational Needs will only make minute steps forward and it is important that these are recorded in some way in order that children, parents and staff and others can understand the progress that has been made.

While it is only natural that change will bring about feelings of uncertainty and resentment, it is hoped that the ideas and suggestions outlined in this chapter will go some way to encourage teachers to realise that Design and Technology is not as 'new' as was first thought. Through the National Curriculum, teachers have now been

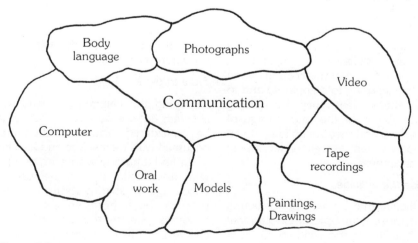

Figure 3.7.4

given a framework within which to work but there is still freedom to decide when and how Technology should be included. Indeed it is important not to lose the spontaneity and creativity that is so often to be found in the classrooms of teachers of Early Years and Special Educational Needs children. If this can be done, it should be possible to carry out still more worthwhile and stimulating projects in the years ahead.

APPENDIX: Resources that might be particularly useful for younger children and those with Special Educational Needs

Waste materials such as boxes of various shapes and sizes, plastic bottles, cylindrical tubes, tins, yoghurt and margarine tubs
Collection of fabrics
Collection of card and papers
Wool and string
Elastic bands
Straws
Pipe cleaners
Clay
Plasticine
Play dough

Dowel and square section soft wood

Children can cut with scissors and a junior hacksaw (a bench hook provides support for the hacksaw).
Fixings could include:
P.V.A. glue
Glue gun (supervised by an adult at all times)
Masking tape
Pipe cleaners
Staples
Paper clips
Split pins (brass paper fasteners)
Drawing pins
Mapping pins
Bulldog clips

COME FLY WITH ME: notes on primary school technology

Richard C. Simpson   *Newcastle upon Tyne Polytechnic*

An episode

The spontaneity of ideas for which young children are well known brings many a precious moment in scientific investigations. For this reason I record an episode of learning first, then I shall discuss how a class of eight and nine year olds embarked on a project about 'Flight'.

A group of ten children, six girls and four boys were set the task of making our plastic lemonade bottle airship 'fly'.

My contribution was to provide the prototype body, pose the initial question, then stand back and see what they came up with to solve the problem.

The group had spent two mornings observing a mounted pigeon wing, some feathers (with a microscope), and a pigeon skeleton.

They had modelled a feather; built a model wing with real feathers, glue and plastic straws; and folded and flown paper aeroplanes.

Later, the children were inspired by a visit from the Norwich Puppet Theatre in which origami was used to great effect, a bird being modelled for use in the play. The children were intrigued and attempted to make origami birds themselves, folding the paper so that the wings moved in the right way.

In the words of the old adage, chance favours the prepared mind, but for me, the greatest excitement of all came from what I had thought would be one of our less exciting adventures.

An earlier group had been frustrated in their experiment by the well known 'balloon rocket' when after a few 'blows up' the balloon burst!

This group had modified the balloon by attacking the straws in the way shown in Fig. 3.8.1 before 'flying' it along the string which we had fixed across the classroom . . . I have to admit this experiment provided an inspired use of the mass of lemonade bottles which littered my study. My idea was that we prevent the balloon from bursting by enclosing it in the lemonade bottle, blowing it up, then letting it go so that the expelled air would force the airship along the track . . . (so much for a lifetime of science education!)

Efforts to blow up the balloon failed miserably, in spite of the valiant efforts of all the children, but especially those of Matthew. Here was a physics problem of seemingly insoluble dimensions in a restricted and meaningful context for the children.

Having been asked the question, 'Why won't the balloon blow up?' their ideas came fast and furious. They understood that they were blowing air from their lungs into it, and that the bottle already contained air . . . but why was the little bottle of air stopping the 'bigger amount of breath?'

Elizabeth suggested that if we could get plasticine inside the balloon, this would make it weigh heavier so that it would push the air in the bottle away, and so the balloon would 'go up'.

James took over (a not unusual situation with boys, the girls often generate the ideas). He patiently introduced bits of plasticine into the balloon, but then had the greatest difficulty in introducing the balloon into the bottle. . . . They still could not manage to inflate the balloon!

'Maybe the plasticine won't work because it's in little pieces,' said Paul.

So they 'lumped' it together by squeezing the balloon . . . still frustration! Matthew, a thoughtful but quiet pupil, said we could blow it up by using a straw. Brady dashed off to another classroom where 'the little ones' had milk, to get some straws. Brady was always the one to produce what was needed.

James tried again and again, others took over, but to no avail.

Matthew: 'It's because the air leaks from the side of the straw!' So he taped it firmly into the neck of the balloon, but only a very limited 'blow up' resulted.

'I know,' said Ailsa, 'we could make a bundle

Fig. 3.8.1. The Model Airship

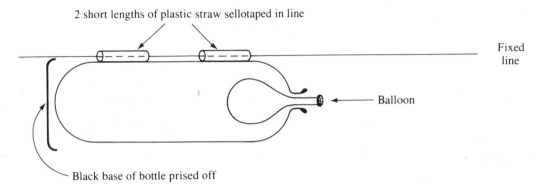

2 short lengths of plastic straw sellotaped in line

Fixed line

Balloon

Black base of bottle prised off

of straws and push it into the neck of the balloon, then seal them in with sellotape.'

Matthew, who had a red face occasioned by his exertions, was elected as Chief Blower. The balloon inflated a bit more this time, but they had not solved the problem to their satisfaction in spite of the cheers! The argument and ideas continued to flow, the excitement of the children was infectious, and at that point I had to leave . . . they did not even notice my going!

I wondered if they would come to a conclusion before my visit next week? I think I can solve the problem now, but will they? Incidentally, I had not thought this experiment would have proved such a problem, but did not come up with an answer until the following day.

The solution should be to let the air out of the bottle in some way . . . it would have been so easy to tell them, but how glad I was that I had not intruded! Here was a truly scientific/ technological problem-solving situation from a simple beginning.

The children hypothesised, predicted outcomes, indulged in explanations, but above all, learnt the very valuable lesson of patient perseverance and co-operation.

One regret was that the 'ideas girls' had become partially excluded by the 'action boys', save for Michael, who though contributing ideas, remained quietly in the background at 'doing' time on this occasion.

Who says 'girls think, boys do' beware of stereotyping! Though certain individuals are

mentioned by name, all the children contributed in an animated way to the solution of the problems, the social skills improving, but learning to co-operate being the most important outcome of all. (Previously Matthew had hogged all the materials on his table when his group was asked to produce a model wing).

What an experience for the children and their teacher!

Organising the problem-solving situations

The class had been organised into groups which took turns for a three to four week period to experiment for a whole morning, a fifth group was located in another class.

The overall objective of the project was to gain an insight into how children would evolve strategies for problem-solving in a technological context. The report just given was of the experiment undertaken by the penultimate group of ten children.

Their class teacher organised the other group activities whilst the chosen group experimented. I make no apologies for this organisation, it is impossible to gain such experience in a whole class situation since the teacher has to be constantly acting as a 'lab technician' when the children demand materials so 'the enabling questions' can rarely be posed. Recipe 'closed science' often seems to be the result of a class science lesson; there is little scope for spontaneity.

The ideas were started by the ancillary teacher (me) who insisted that the children always sat down with pencil and paper and 'designed' things before they were allowed to 'do things'.

This in itself is a valuable exercise, committing thoughts to paper through drawing. The inevitable 'I can't draw' came up, but with encouragement, it was amazing how proficient the children became at 'engineering drawing' though one must hasten to add, not what our secondary colleagues would regard as such. The reservation rarely occurred more than once with a particular child. Every group was given its own unique experience though they might be repeated with different groups.

The work was concluded with the whole class reporting, group by group, what they had found out. A spokesperson was chosen for each group . . . though others managed to have their say.

And finally, we all flew our lemonade bottle airship together on a line across the whole length of the mobile classroom.

I hope this convinces you that technology in the primary school is inexpensive, possible for both pupils and teacher alike, and can add a unique dimension to children's learning, ie *Design, Build, Test*.

It really does not need microcomputers or expensive commercial kits. These are useful extensions rather than essential materials.

If you feel you've heard it before, I agree, it was called primary science. Technology for me is not materials, accurate use of forbidding tools and 'write it up', it's about children thinking on their feet about *design, taking decisions, and doing it*.

What have the children achieved in scientific/technological terms?

Skills/Strategies

1. Accurate observation/looking carefully, drawing.
2. Predicting outcomes/Can you think/guess what might happen if?
3. Identifying a problem/*What* might we do here?
4. Making decisions/*How* might we do it?
5. *Designing* a solution – individual/group discussion. Drawing.
6. *Building* a device/Doing it! Use of simple tools.
7. *Testing* to see if it works/*How* can we find out? *Why* do this? A 'fair test'.
8. Manipulation of simple tools and materials . . . paper, card, plastic, wood, foil, sellotape, glue, Pritstick, colouring tools, scissors, craft knife (incidentally, the girls were far su-

perior to the boys in their use of tools. Much more accurate cutters).

And what have they learnt socially?
1. To wait their turn in discussion and in test situations.
2. To work on co-operative ventures.
3. To reject 'poor' efforts, theirs or other people's, and to select the best.
4. To take failure in their stride and start again.
5. To take pride in persevering with a job and in the result however 'humble'.
6. To try things out for themselves at home.
7. Patience when following verbal instructions.
8. To enjoy technology.
9. The need for safe practice.

And have yet again been an inspiration to their teachers. Success is a powerful motivator and morale booster. Have a go . . . I'm sure you'll enjoy it too.

P.S. They practised their basic skills in a relevant context for them.

Some avenues explored in our theme – 'Flying Things'

Group 1
Four boys and two girls. Starting point: a walk to gather seeds.

Technology starters:
What is a seed?
Why can some seeds fly?
Can you *design* a good flying seed using only card and plasticine?
What parts does it need?
How are you going to make seeds?
Whose flies the best and *why*?

Other areas:
Building models.
Germination experiments (not done).
Chart of seed types (made by children).
Chart of flying words (suggested by children).
Looking at a 'helicopter' tree seed and watching it fly (the tree was a sycamore).
Designing and flying a paper helicopter.
A squeezy bottle water rocket.

I suspect that they enjoyed it best when the end of the water rocket burst and soaked the teacher!

Group 2
Ten children, four girls and six boys. Starting point: A toy card boomerang.

Technology:
Getting it to fly.
Can you make a better one?
Design your own.

Other areas:
Drawing and design.
A running line rocket (see Aerial models)
What was a boomerang used for?
How was it used?
Who used it?
A discussion about Aborigines . . . story written about a hunting trip.
World Airway routes from Australia . . . a quiz game using an atlas.

Group 3
Five children, two boys and three girls. Starting point: a real boomerang, borrowed from Newcastle Polytechnic Museum.

Technology:
Why was it this shape?
Can you make one as good in another shape?
How would you use it?
Why does it have a kangaroo carving on it?
Design and make a balsa boomerang (used balsa, glue and pins, and craft knives)
Whose flies the furthest?
Can you get it to come back? (Wendy solved this)
Old and new aeroplane shapes. Why are these different? Slow/fast fliers.
Designing a plane, not from a plan (shapes made in plasticine and they looked down on them).
Make and fly a cardboard plane.
Which flew best?
What did 'best' mean?
Could they suggest *why*?
Modify your design to improve performance.
One of the boys made a gull winged plane which did remarkable aerobatics.

Group 4
Ten children, four boys and six girls. Starting point: Birds as flying machines – looking at a feather, a wing, a bird skeleton.

Technology:
Why do birds have feathers?
Are they the same?
Why is the feather disrupted if we stroke it the wrong way? So *what* holds them together?
How are feathers arranged on a wing?
Why is this arrangement best?
Make a model feather from card and a straw.
Name the kinds and parts of a feather.
Wing bones, *why* are they arranged as they are?
(X ray photo . . . from Newcastle Polytechnic Library)
Make a model wing using real feathers, and straws to simulate bones.

Other areas:
Design a wing.
An origami bird.
The incredible flying tube (thick paper). Figure 2.

A paper plane (to my surprise, they did not know how to make one) and, best of all, the lemonade bottle airship!

Group 5
Two girls and seven boys (in progress). Starting point: our Spaceship crashed on an unknown planet.

Technology:
What is needed on a spaceship?
What does a space rocket look like?
What does a planet's surface look like?

Fig. 3.8.2. The Incredible Flying Tube

 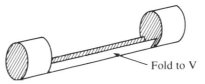

Fold to V

Make a tube at each end
and glue ends together

What would we need to survive?

A moon map was used to assist imagination.

Other areas:

We need to go from the crash point to the Sea of Happiness . . . plot your route (draw a map). It's a long way, so *how* are we going to get there?

This is where the space vehicle will be designed and built. Hope to use control technology. Looking at rocks and fossils (these were real specimens but they had to *use their imagination* to attribute them to an unknown planet).

Sources of ideas

Phillips Picture Atlas – world airway routes.

Schools Council (1978) Teaching Primary Science Project: Aerial Models. Macdonald.

Standing Conference on Schools' Science & Technology (1984). Science and Technology in the Primary School, SCSST.

West Sussex Science 5–14 Project (1983). Science Horizons: Flying Things. West Sussex CC.

Dedicated to the children of Classes 1 and 2, Broadway East First School, Newcastle upon Tyne, whose enthusiasm was so infectious, and whose ideas were so ingenious.

SOLVING PROBLEMS IN SCIENCE

Nicola S. Gilbert *student-teacher, King Alfred's College, Winchester*

In the DES report *'Science 5–16 : A statement of policy'* it is stated that, ' . . . science is a practical subject, and should be taught at all stages in a way which emphasises practical, investigative and problem-solving activity; . . .' Unfortunately for the teacher there are no practical suggestions as to how this problem-solving and discovery process is to be undertaken.

This issue was brought to the attention of a group of teacher-training students at King Alfred's College in Winchester. We decided to go into a local school, put the theory into practice, and find out whether it could form a realistic policy for the teaching of science.

The findings of our study were not all positive. Having realised the importance of knowing what not to do, as well as what works, I shall discuss both positive and negative aspects of our experience. I hope this will leave the reader with a series of suggestions, as well as some general guidelines for further science topics.

Our group selected a topic of *WIND* and, in order to study its physical aspects, decided to follow a series of activities aimed at enabling the children to design and build their own kites.

The initial visit was begun by a discussion, to discover how much the children already knew.

Key questions:
How do you know when it's windy outside?
Does the wind change? How?
How strong is the wind?
(The central ideas extracted from this were those of speed, direction, power and wind-resistance.)

We then passed round a selection of junk materials and different types of cloth and asked the children to test them to see which types of things flew well.

In order to define the problem the children were given two key phrases to work with.
"Catching the wind" – increasing wind resistance to a maximum.
"Cutting the wind" – reducing wind resistance to a minimum.
The children had to attempt to do both these things with each item; and then see the result of combining these effects in some way. They worked in small groups or pairs and the interaction between these groups (comparing results, demonstrating interesting effects etc.) was particularly valuable. They discovered ways of holding the material in order to:

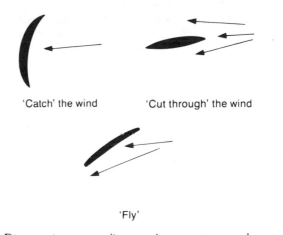

'Catch' the wind   'Cut through' the wind

'Fly'

Discoveries were discussed as a class and applied by the construction of model parachutes. The children were given their choice of materials and asked to design the models in pairs. These were modelled around commercial brands and were obviously successful. Unfortunately the children had entirely failed to reason for themselves – or to take into account the discoveries they had made earlier that morning. The reason for this phenomenon was blindingly obvious, once perceived. The discoveries made with the materials pointed towards 'flight' being a combination of air resistance and aerodynamic lift: by this definition parachutes don't 'fly' at all: as we can see from the two diagrams below.

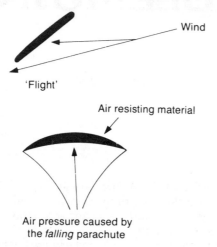

'Flight'

Wind

Air resisting material

Air pressure caused by the *falling* parachute

The moral of this story is that the problem solving exercise must be directly and obviously applicable to any previous discoveries, or the children may be confused by the change of direction, discard the previous information as useless, and give up any attempt to reason for themselves.

In order to counteract this confusion the children were once again set a basic, discovery-orientated task. They were given identical pieces of paper, which they raced by blowing them along the floor. They were then invited to alter their paper in any way they chose – the aim being to improve their chances of winning. The alterations were discussed as a class in the light of their performance. The most successful designs were found to have both horizontal and vertical surfaces; as well as a large surface area for 'catching' the air current. This activity was particularly successful – both in terms of its primary objective and in the interest it evoked.

It was at this stage that the children were asked to begin constructing 'proper kites'. It had been noticed that some of the children had very little previous experience with practical tasks. As kite-building requires some fairly advanced manual skills it was decided to simplify the problem by the construction of solid state kites (ie kites constructed from a single, cut out shape which do not require struts.) Since we had noted the tendency to base designs on commercial models, the children were prevented from all making identical diamond shaped kites by being given a specific shape to work with (eg triangle, circle, square etc. NB. It is important that these shapes are symmetrical).

The materials provided were basically corrugated card (old boxes) and polystyrene slabs. Understandably drawn by the polystyrene, most groups constructed their kites of this initially. However, the slabs were so thick that they hardly flew at all. Having failed to solve the problem 'correctly' most of the children either asked us how to do it 'right' or gave up.

> 'It broke, we had to go and mend it but it broke again so now I don't know what to do.' (Leanne)

The children apparently had no concept of the scientific cycle of experimentation and improvement, they were totally geared to things working first time.

In an attempt to change this attitude, we asked the children to complete sheets such as the one below during the construction of their kites.

Stage of Kite (diagram/materials)	Experiment (what happened)	Analysis (why did it happen?)	Ideas for improvement
i)			
ii)			

Once explained, these sheets proved to be incredibly successful. The children finally realised that they were allowed to alter previous decisions/designs in order to solve their problems. They began to request different materials (this only being allowed if they could present a good case for needing it) and more sophisticated designs began to appear. As the need for lighter materials became apparent, so did the need for struts to hold the material taut. The use of tails was investigated, in order to stop the kite spinning; and various methods were invented to prevent the strings tangling. The individuality of the ways in which they solved their design problems was shown in the variety of the finished kites.

EXAMPLES OF DESIGNS FOR KITES

Two variations on the wind-sock

Lee and Scott

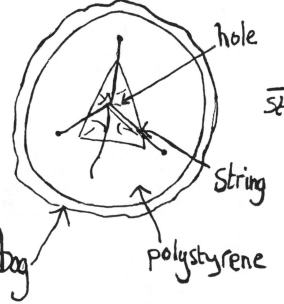

(side view)

(front view)

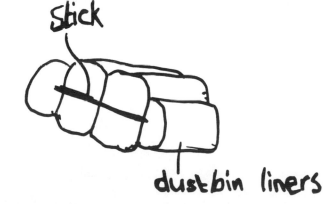

Jamie

A variation on the box kite: Pamela & Michelle

Emma & Hayley's Hexagonal kite
– it is flown by two people to increase its stability

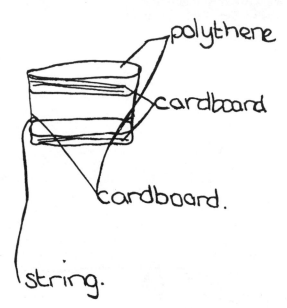

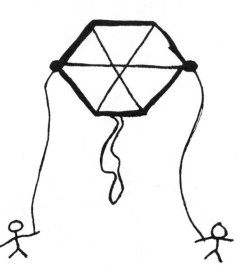

At the end of our time with the children, we concluded that investigative and problem solving learning can be used very successfully as a teaching strategy. There are, however, a number of points which have to be kept in mind:

(i) This approach takes up a good deal of time and effort – activities should be done in small groups and the results reported to the class.

(ii) The standard of the work is directly related to the variety and suitability of the materials provided.

(iii) The scientific process is blocked by the 'first time mentality' of most children: and has to be explicitly demonstrated before they are likely to grasp its significance.

(iv) Basic skills inherent in this type of work should be fostered in other subject areas (eg the problems faced with forming shapes could have led to a maths lesson in simple geometry)

Most importantly – don't worry if things don't turn out quite the way you planned them. Such things are bound to happen once the children begin to think for themselves.

STARTING SCIENCE AND TECHNOLOGY FROM JUNK

Steve Marshall *advisory teacher for science and technology, London Borough of Barnet LEA*

Children learn when they can see a purpose to the activity, exploration, investigation, or problem in which they are engaged. So, in theory, 'there is no real problem for teachers in their planning strategy'. Unfortunately for the theory, children are individuals, each being quite unique. A particular context for one child may very well bear little meaning for the next. Should we impose identical contexts for all children, or should we be preparing individual programmes of learning? The answer must be closely related to the latter, but if it does what effect will this have on the class teacher?

At one extreme, it will mean a class of 30, having 30 quite separate programmes. Although well meaning, it is unmanageable and restrictive for the very children we are trying to help. Probably much more manageable and beneficial for those children is a grouped approach to the programmes. Here we can have a theme for the class and children grouped in order to follow a smaller number of pathways. At the other extreme we can move the whole class forward together as one unit. Each system has its supporters and doubters. Each system supports different purposes and teaching styles at different times. As teachers we need to be aware of each strategy and be ready to implement any method at the appropriate time. We must be ready to grab hold of any opportunity and make informed decisions as to the degree of meaning and purpose of any activity. The chance may arise in the form of an off-the-cuff observation; 'A ground frost on the way to school this morning.' A statement such as, 'My coat keeps me dry'. Maybe a question; 'Why do hot things freeze before cold things?' An appearance of an object in school, for whatever reason, e.g. a favourite toy or souvenir

from a holiday or day out. We must be ready to seize upon these opportunities, which have immediate meaning and purpose for our children but at the same time be aware of the role such activities may play in the overall scheme of work for the children.

I recount here, therefore, a situation that arose in school before the National Curriculum was fully known about, and try now to look at how the work might have developed in the light of the attainment targets and programmes of study in Science and Design and Technology.

The school collection of 'junk' had grown quite considerably over the year and with the Summer half term approaching it was time to have a major clear out and tidy up. During this process a large box of those plastic film canisters was discovered (approximately 100). It seemed a shame to throw away all that plastic, but was there anything we could use it for? A challenge was set for the children. 'What uses can we make of these little containers?' Within half an hour we had over 50 suggestions, mostly for use in the classroom in the form of teaching aids, activities or general use. By the end of half-term, brainstorming with people in all sorts of situations led to 101 uses, and provided the basis of the final topic for the year. The children would concentrate their work around the little containers. On the following pages are six examples of the uses the containers were put to, selected to illustrate those that particularly contribute to learning in science and technology.

These were interesting activities, but what was missing was a sound way of seeing what aspects of the school curriculum were being engaged, and what aspects of science and technology were being experienced.

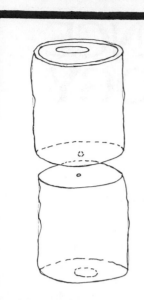

DESIGNING TIMERS

1. Take two transparent film canisters, and using a hand drill and bit put a hole through the base of each.
Put the hole through from the inside in each.

2. Ensure that the holes are correctly lined up. Using sticky tape secure the two canisters together.

3. Place the lid on one canister.

4. Pour in salt/dry sand to the other canister.

5. Secure the second lid.

6. Invert the timer and watch the sand pour through to the lower container.

7. Sometimes the edges of the holes need tidying, use a rat-tail file.

EXTENSION

1. Can the timer be made to last 10s/15s?

2. What effect does increasing the hole size have?

3. What happens if there is more than one hole?

4. Can a device be made to allow easy turning?

5. Could larger/longer timers be made?

ROLLING LIQUIDS

1. Partly fill 5 clear canisters with liquid. Select a different liquid for each container ie. water, cooking oil, shampoo, liquid soap, glycerine.

2. For the pupils:
Look carefully at the 5 liquids. What are the differences and similarities between them? Take each container and lay it down on its side. Do you notice anything about the liquid inside? Record your observations.

3. Now roll them down a slope. What do you notice? Measure how long it takes each container to roll down.

4. Is there a rule? Do they all obey this rule?

EXTENSION

1. Test other liquids.

2. Does the steepness of slope have any affect?

3. Other rollers.

4. Different quantities of the same liquid.

5. Different contents ie. sand, talcum powder, flour.

6. Rolling toys – eg film canister tanks.

Figure 3.10.1

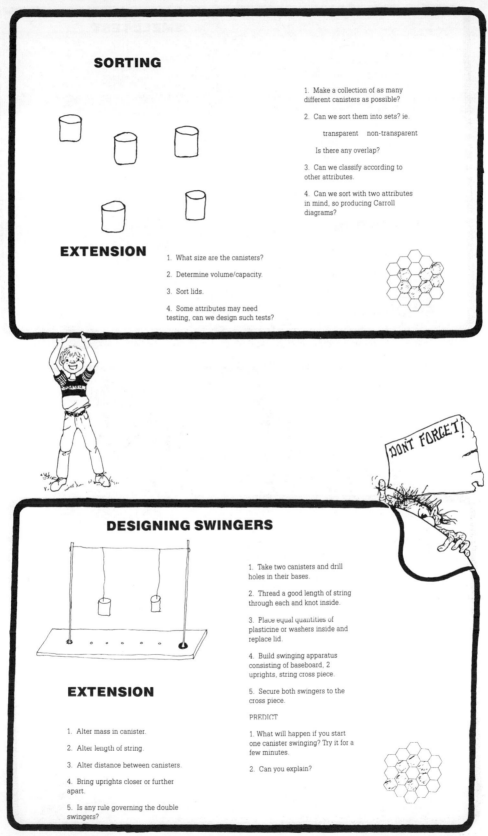

SORTING

1. Make a collection of as many different canisters as possible?

2. Can we sort them into sets? ie.

     transparent   non-transparent

   Is there any overlap?

3. Can we classify according to other attributes.

4. Can we sort with two attributes in mind, so producing Carroll diagrams?

EXTENSION

1. What size are the canisters?

2. Determine volume/capacity.

3. Sort lids.

4. Some attributes may need testing, can we design such tests?

DESIGNING SWINGERS

1. Take two canisters and drill holes in their bases.

2. Thread a good length of string through each and knot inside.

3. Place equal quantities of plasticine or washers inside and replace lid.

4. Build swinging apparatus consisting of baseboard, 2 uprights, string cross piece.

5. Secure both swingers to the cross piece.

PREDICT

1. What will happen if you start one canister swinging? Try it for a few minutes.

2. Can you explain?

EXTENSION

1. Alter mass in canister.

2. Alter length of string.

3. Alter distance between canisters.

4. Bring uprights closer or further apart.

5. Is any rule governing the double swingers?

Figure 3.10.2

SMELL TEST

1. Place small quantity of cotton wool in the base of a non-clear canister.
2. Add a few drops of liquid smell source onto cotton wool.
3. Use a canister lid to seal in odour/smell.
4. Label canister with appropriate number or letter.
5. If using solids to create smell then cover with cotton wool, to keep in place.
6. Remember safety points regarding smells 'only those things for which permission is given'.
7. When smelling remove lid and waft smell towards nose using hand. Do not thrust nose into canister.
8. Encourage recording in the form of like/dislike, or what does it remind you of? It is difficult to actually name smells.

Possible smell sources:-
vinegar, almond essence, vanilla, brandy flavour, ketchup, coffee.

EXTENSION

1. How strong is a smell?
Put 1, 2, 3 holes in lid.
How far away can it be detected?

2. Can you design smell proof containers?

3. Does smell affect taste?

SCIENCE OR MAGIC?

1. Take one canister, put 6 paper clips in and strap to your left wrist. Cover with shirt etc.

2. Place 3 other canisters on table. Using right hand lift 2 canisters one at a time and shake. They are empty. The left hand shakes the third canister, which appears to contain something.

3. Switch canisters on table into a new order. Which one has something in?

4. Show they are wrong by shaking with the appropriate hand, then show which has the contents with appropriate shaking.

5. Repeat the shuffle.

6. Brainstorm how the trick is achieved.

7. Can the children repeat the trick?

8. In Science and Technology we need to observe & identify patterns.

9. 'A canister only has something in it when shaken by the left hand'.

Figure 3.10.3

In the light of the National Curriculum this identification has become easier especially when approached through the hexagons that follow (see Fig. 3.10.4).

brings together the individual ATs from science. When we reach this level in our planning, it is necessary to refer to the Programmes of Study. It will now be possible to see what aspects of the

HEXAGONS

level 1 aspects,

plan, carry out, communicate, hypothesise, interpret, knowledge & understanding contribute to the process of Science & Technology.

level 2 aspects,

noise, shape, colour, inside/outside, materials, size, aspects of the resource item that can be considered for explorations, ie. How big is it? What is it made of? Can it move? Does it make noises? What colour, shape is it?

level 3 aspects,

the Attainment Targets/Programmes of Study.

Use: levels 1 & 2 are free to rotate, so as to highlight unexpected aspects, ie. using canisters as light bulb holders/shields.

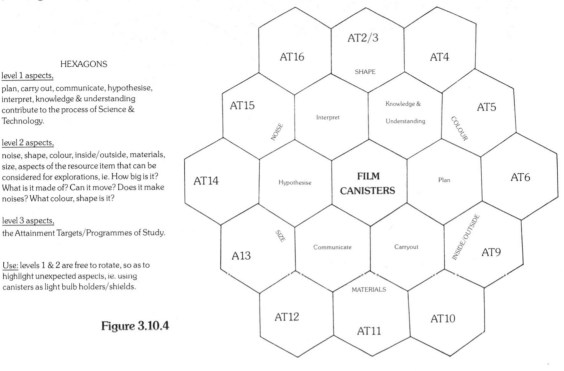

Figure 3.10.4

The orders for *Science in the National Curriculum* divide the area of science into two Profile Components (PC). The one PC with Attainment Target (AT) 1 'Exploration of Science' must play an important part when planning science work, experiences and activities. The consultation report on Design and Technology in the National Curriculum places emphasis on 'capability' rather than knowledge; that is on being able to 'operate effectively and creatively in the made world'[1]. It is this 'process and doing' that is close to the heart of the Hexagons. A glance will show that at the heart is the topic or theme, in this case plastic film canisters. As we move out to the first level we are reminded of the Exploration of Science, the skills and processes involved in 'Being a Scientist'. Included here is the knowledge and understanding, mainly as a reminder that facts and concepts do play a valued part in science, but the detailed knowledge and understanding appears later in the planning process.

The next level of the Hexagons reminds us of the aspects we can consider for developing children's explorations. More detail of this can be seen in the individual explorations and activities already described. The final level of Hexagons

National Curriculum are being covered and which aspects of the whole school curriculum are being experienced (see Fig. 3.10.5).

Other ideas for work in the Science and Design Technology area of the curriculum using the plastic film canisters:

1 Battery holder (C size)
2 Cotton reel tanks
3 Seed germination pots
4 Cress seed growing
5 Bulb holder for traffic lights
6 Spinning tops
7 Push/pull meter
8 Butter making
9 Buoyancy aids in boat building
10 Sand displays

The canisters provided the source of many fun topics with many serious applications. The children enjoyed it, the work was relevant, meaningful and with purpose. I have deliberately illustrated explorations and activities that might be thought of as science and technology, because for most primary schools it will be helpful to extend their science activities to include design, rather than to think of them as different and unrelated.

National Curriculum is only a part of the whole school curriculum. It is the outer ring that makes each school special.

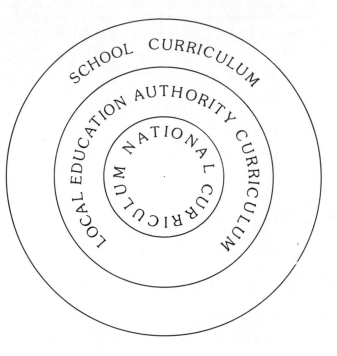

Figure 3.10.5

As well as the rewards for the children, it was rewarding for me to see how such a seemingly mundane and useless piece of 'junk' could in fact become a most valuable science and technology resource.

Reference

[1] Department of Education and Science (1989) *National Curriculum, Design and Technology Working Group, Final Report.* HMSO.

RAISING BARRIERS WITH CONTROL TECHNOLOGY

Rod Buckle   *Springhead School, Scarborough*

Control technology and children's learning

The computer has become an integral piece of school equipment in recent years and has had an effect on teaching and learning methodology across many areas of the primary curriculum. Most of these curricular areas have used micro-technology in the development of computer assisted learning strategies. With the introduction of alternative strategies in secondary education such as TVEI projects and the current concern shown by the DES and others about the lack of emphasis placed on science and vocationally oriented curriculum areas, we are being encouraged to look at ways of developing other areas of technologically-based learning within the primary school. The development of control technology in primary schools promises to fill all the required criteria emphasised in the recommended areas but may contain inherent and far reaching implications for the pupil/teacher relationship. In the traditional educational framework we all too often tend to present pupils with a contrived learning experience that bears little relation to the real situation which exists outside the school. We expect problems to be solved within a time limit and with a predetermined 'correct' solution. Each problem tends to be approached by the individual child, who is often expected to solve the problem using only the information given by the teacher.

Control technology involves the pupil in using first hand experiences and it is cross-curricular in nature. It is appropriate for children of all ages and abilities. Mistakes are not seen as failures, only as experiences to use to develop a working solution. The mistakes provide feedback about the next step to take in the process. This search for a workable solution can be described as debugging. This is a term used in computing to describe the process of removing the factors which are preventing us from arriving at a working solution to a programming problem. The fear of 'getting it wrong' vanishes and we learn from our mistakes and not continue to suffer for them.

Children should become self correcting individuals.

The teacher's relationship with the pupil in control technology is greatly changed. However, the support of sensitive and observant adults is vital because the more open-ended the learning tool, the more chance the child has to extend his/her power. There is also an increased chance of the child becoming frustrated and confused. In the present educational system the act of teaching still tends to hold the position of highest priority as opposed to the act of learning. Within control technology the role of the teacher shifts from that of instructor to that of consultant. Some teachers may find this shift in role difficult, others may even feel threatened as they are confronted by the fact that children can acquire considerable expertise with computers and equipment. It is not easy to become a partner in discovery and many teachers will feel insecure. Working with computers and control technology will often mean that it is counter productive for the teacher to simply tell the child what the problem is, as a large percentage of the learning may be lost this way. This will require a curriculum approach where the unexpected is valued and unanticipated ideas from the children encouraged.

It is likely that in future children will be capable of creating a much wider range of generalisation based on their own first hand experience and from readily available information. They may be able to determine their own ways of classifying their world around them rather than accepting predetermined and possibly misunderstood classifications. Our methodologies may have to be evaluated when we realise the consequences of interactive learning. The interaction between the child setting and solving their own problems allows the teacher to match the task to the learner more accurately. The motivational benefits of self-directed learning enable the most able child to be unconstrained by anything other than hardware limitations. The less able child is able to experience achievement resulting from the motivation enabled by an interactive learning activity unprecedented in normal academic subjects where you are right or wrong and in the case of the less able they are often wrong.

By encouraging the child to control machines we are reducing the possibility of any fear of technology which affects some adults (including teachers). Aspects of competition may be modified by the child setting his/her own goals, and invariably experiencing a co-operative situation rather than a competitive one.

Control technology in practice

I became involved with a local primary school, whose teachers were already committed to the development of computer assisted learning across the curriculum, and who had indicated an intention to introduce control technology within the school. The school had three computers and as all were in constant use throughout the school it appeared safe to assume that the majority members of staff were committed to the use of computers on a regular basis within the classroom situation. (See Appendix A for the equipment used). It is important that both children and teachers should have developed a comfortable relationship with the computer over a period of time. This is important for the teachers involved because as well as the essential confidence in both their own and the computer's capabilities they should have come to accept that good exposition by the teacher is not a monologue but a series of questions asked by the teacher and responded to by the children. The role of the teacher in encouraging discussion about the possible forms of solution is an important one in helping to extend the children's thinking about a particular problem. This role can only be fulfilled by the teachers if they have ceased to be concerned about the basic operations needed to communicate with the computer. The biggest contribution the micro can make to the classroom comes from encouraging children to use the computer creatively by commanding it to carry out instructions. During a process of investigation children are encouraged to conjecture, to test their theories and draw generalised conclusions.

The first sessions were with the top juniors (Y6) which consisted of a class of 28 children including 3 children from the special behavioural needs unit attached to the school. As the class were already involved in a project looking at change it was decided to use the development of the machines used in the home as a starting point. The sessions were to occupy one after-

noon per week with a mid-afternoon break; any shorter time span could lead to the abandonment of the child's design processes before completion which may be highly discouraging for the child and unproductive towards the basic aims of introducing control technology. The first part of the session (approximately 15 minutes) was spent introducing the general topic of technology. The interface which connects the output and input devices to the computer was demonstrated and the necessary keywords were explained. These were written on a reference chart which was fixed on the wall. Children selected themselves into groups of four. Initially the groups were restricted to using the words needed to switch on and off output devices in direct mode, (by pressing a key rather than by a procedure). It was at this point that the realisation dawned that any formulated time scale for the introduction of ideas was likely to be on a different continuum to the children's. The class began to ask questions about controlling outputs remotely as the machines we had been discussing were in the home situation (washing machines etc.). They went away to write some short procedures (programs) to operate the lights, buzzers and other output devices. There were two forms of the Logo language available for the children to use when writing their procedures. One was a simplified version which was supplied by the manufacturers of the control interface box and the other was a more complex and 'full' implementation of the language developed by Logotron. It was decided that as this was to be a long term project that would become a permanent part of the school curriculum it would be beneficial for the more complex developments envisaged if we introduced the more comprehensive version of the language in the initial stages. This would also mean that the children would use the same 'language' to drive the Valiant Turtle as well as Logo projects throughout the school once these activities were established. Once the procedures had been written down on paper in note form the groups came and tested them on the computer. If the procedures worked then they were written in their individual files; if there were 'bugs' in the procedures then the group went away to rethink their ideas (with teacher help if requested). The first session ended by a 'de-briefing' period where the groups announced their findings and some of the main keywords were repeated and the functions of output devices were reinforced.

During the following week the children made various models of household machines that could be operated by switches. The children used Technical Lego to build their models and

recorded their designs via a mixture of diagrams, pictures and text which were placed in their files alongside pictures of the real object extracted from magazines etc. The children designed procedures away from the computer to enable them to control their devices via the interface box. When they had tested their procedures on the computer they were typed into a second computer and a copy printed out for them to place in their files as a record. Devices built included:
- A four wheel drive lawn mower with an engine and an indicator light to show when the motor was switched on.
- A fan, a washing machine, a food mixer all of which operated and had an indicator light.

The children began to destroy any plans we may have had for dictating the speed of progression when two girls approached with a query. They had built a washing machine and had realised that it revolved too quickly. They wished to know how to slow it down. Before I could reply, a boy in another group suggested they had some gears 'like on his bike'. The girls were shown diagrams of simple gearing systems and had the basic principles explained to them. They went off clutching the Lego manual and frantically discussing whether they should go 'big' to 'small' or the other way round with their cog arrangement. This was one of the most disconcerting aspects of this type of learning situation. Once the children had begun to control the direction their learning was to go in they were very reluctant to give it back. Even though I had seen this as a desirable aspect of introducing control technology I still found the situation unnerving after years of dictating the pace of children's learning. It was apparent that I had made an error when placing children in groups of four. These groups were too big as it appeared to lead to some children sitting back and allowing others to dominate the design process. Reducing the group size to three alleviated this problem.

It became apparent to the children that there was more than one workable solution to most problems. This was heavily emphasised during a child's period for recording their work. The children were encouraged to record their 'mistakes' as often these were important in their thought processes in finding a workable solution. All through the project the children were encouraged to look on mistakes as useful tools for re-directing their thinking rather than something they should be reticent to talk about.

The designing and building activities took place away from the computer. The children were already dictating their own pace with some children working on challenges, some testing their procedures for household devices, and others using the word processor on the second computer for recording activities.

The children were shown how to build their procedures in the 'edit' mode available using the Logotron full version of Logo. This enabled them to alter and extend procedures much more easily. This was becoming essential as their procedures were becoming more complex as they were solving problems of a greater complexity. A computer disk was set aside as a library disk and the children saved their procedures onto the disk. They also made a note of their procedures' names on a reference card on the wall. This would ensure that names were not repeated and therefore other people's work should not then be accidentally corrupted. A note of what the procedure did was added to the card and along with a small number of simple procedures which had been used to demonstrate switches, a library of procedures and routines were built up. This would help to prevent children spending time 'reinventing the wheel'. It was becoming clear that sometimes the challenges, once begun, began to lead to other ideas and other problems. Two girls working on the problem of an automatic lighthouse decided that if the light was to work by a light sensor detecting when darkness fell then it would be more efficient if the lighthouse revolved to follow the sun. They began to look at gearing methods and ways of making things revolve. A group of boys extended the design of a burglar alarm to include a panel of three different coloured lights. By using three separate input devices they could tell where the intruder had entered the building. They drew a diagram with the panel mounted in a security office with a pressure pad to detect anyone coming through the door of the main building and two separate light sensors covering a window and skylight. These sensors were then connected to different coloured light bulbs. Not all children found the self-direction or the problem-solving process comfortable initially, but with an adult to suggest occasional clues and act as a catalyst all the group were by now working at a fairly high level of their potential and with great enjoyment.

As the children's voyages of discovery began to vanish over the horizon the lack of hardware became a problem. Despite much of the work being done away from the computer the time needed using the control interface to test hypotheses increased in direct proportion to the complexity of the ideas. The initial enthusiasm shown by the girls in the class had been maintained and in some cases enhanced. The pupils with learning difficulties entered into the design and building exercises enthusiastically. They had creative ideas and often the main task of the teacher seemed to be keeping their ideas within a practical framework to enable the pupil to develop their hypothesis into a working model. The frustration and lack of purpose tended to occur when the time came to record their experiments. This was often alleviated by encouraging the recording procedures to be based on a diagrammatical format. Ideas do not necessarily need to be recorded in a text-only format and all the group were encouraged to look at the most efficient way of communicating information with others. Where children with learning difficulties could not record in a graphic form they often solved the problem for themselves by passing their ideas to another child and getting that child to do the recording for them. The pupils with special needs tended to need to be able to associate their projects closely with reality and to be based on concrete situations. One of the boys with special needs began working on a food mixer that could be operated via a pressure pad to enable it to be used by a handicapped person.

Implications for teachers

If we are to produce innovation in education we should be prepared to fulfill a responsibility to the demands of the educational tradition of evaluation. There is a problem in evaluating a child who produces a mundane but completed solution with little effort whilst another child may have followed an exciting line of development and worked hard but did not actually produce a finished solution. The child must be encouraged to undertake a process of self evaluation. A child should be encouraged to keep a folder containing their designs and solutions as a tool for self evaluation. It is important that children record the thinking processes they have been through in coming to the solution. The file should contain their notes and diagrams done during the investigative stages, some notes made during the solving process mentioning their errors and how they were overcome as well as any solutions they may have arrived at. Their procedures should be included along with any application they can see for their designs in the 'real' world. It was apparent during the introduction process that where the children were expected to evaluate their own work their standards tended to be higher than the teachers.

Control technology has a number of advantages that are apparent within a very short space of time of implementation in the classroom situation. Immediately the value of offering first hand practical experiences to young children becomes obvious. The use of the computer follows as a natural consequence of these practical experi-

ences, and this helps children to formulate concepts and to the use of technology in a relaxed and natural way. Control technology provides an excellent vehicle for problem solving activities with small groups of children. It could be suggested that there is a scarcity of educational situations within the primary curriculum which can offer the possibilities of guided discovery and the encouragement of applying logical thinking in problem solving activities. The scientific and mathematical relationships are developed in a realistic/practical context and are seen by the children as being relevant to their needs. Control technology offers a stimulating way of developing process skills such as decision making, evaluation and communicating ideas with others. It also offers a useful link between the concrete experiences required by young children and the more abstract forms of learning.

During classroom activity it was interesting to note that when the children worked in groups it appeared that although they entered into discussions with other members of the group they reverted back to working on an individual basis when involved in the thinking processes. This observation was also made by Galton during the Oracle project[1], who noted (p152):

> 'Pupils are only organised in one or more seated groups for the various activities undertaken, with few exceptions they then work largely alone as individuals. The setting is socialised but the work is individualised'.

Although much concern has been expressed recently about the lack of involvement of girls in the technological areas of the curriculum, it did not appear the case with control technology. The girls involved in the project group were highly enthusiastic and appeared to be confident in their approach to all the technological applications involved. Nor were there any indications that their enthusiasm and commitment were likely to diminish over a period of time. However, the school involved with the project has never suggested to any group of children that they are likely to be more successful when using the computer as a learning tool than any other group, so the girls had already used technology for a considerable period of their school life.

There are problems in the introduction of control technology which need to be considered. Firstly there is a need for considerable staff input, certainly during the initial stages, but this should diminish as the children take more control over the direction of their own learning. Teachers are needed to monitor subsequent group activities and be ready to intervene in the work of each group when this is educationally necessary or desirable. The children needed an answer to a query immediately to maintain their momentum. They needed to share their enthusiasm over both their successes and what they had discovered by their failures at that moment in time. The very nature of a number of groups undertaking different activities around the room means that camouflage is available for the child who may be adept at avoiding work situations. Secondly it is essential that the staff involved have some expertise in the use of all aspects of control technology. This does not mean that they need to be an expert (if such an animal exists!) but they need to have the confidence to cope with either software or hardware problems. Obviously if children cannot get their procedures to work after designing a system then it would clearly be undesirable to allow them to become disillusioned, especially in the early stages of the project when a word of advice or encouragement could direct them into a more productive area of experimentation.

Following the introductory period the response from the children has been impressive and the school is to extend the introduction of control technology into every class and age group throughout the school. As Forrester[2] (p222) describes it:

'It's a mutual doorway. The barriers between adult and child, between teacher and student are broken, and it's person to person. Nobody's looking down on anyone; they are looking each other right in the eye'.

My only fear is that this change in the pupil/teacher relationship may be threatened by the production of commercially produced and packaged control technology 'schemes' which dictate the 'best way' forward and suggest the orderly progression through a number of stages. Rather than raise any barriers this development would be likely to bring them firmly down.

References

[1] Galton M., Simon B. and Croll P. (1982). *Inside the Primary Classroom*, London, Routledge and Kegan Paul.
[2] Forrester T. (1985), *The Information Technology Revolution*, Oxford, Blackwell.

Appendix A: Equipment

3 BBC model B computers
All fitted with Logotron Logo Roms.
One fitted with Wordwise Plus word processing Rom.
1 Epson FX 80 printer.
3 Driver control interface packages.
Supplied by B.E.P.L
362 Spring Road,
Sholing,
Southampton SO2 7PB.
1 Valiant Turtle.
1 Bigtrak.

COMPUTERS IN THE NURSERY

Caroline Matusiak *nursery teacher, Braeburn Infant School, Scarborough*

The use of computers, particularly in nursery classes with access to school facilities, is gradually increasing. Large independent nursery units are also starting to invest in them.

In an organisation of free choice for children from 3 to 5 years, it was the children from about 3 years 10 months to 5 years who showed most interest in computer activities. After all, using a computer requires appropriate handling of equipment, adhering to simple rules and working initially under adult direction. The 3 year olds continually chose tactile activities such as finger paint, wet sand and water, rather than the alternative of pressing keys for visual stimulus. Some children have access to computers at home, and certainly most are familiar with gleaning information from a screen, albeit a television screen.

The three areas I examined were the use of ready-made nursery programs, word-processing and the concept keyboard. This revealed useful insights into children's attempts to understand computer literacy. It cannot necessarily be assumed, however, that the use of computers in the nursery is educationally viable and worthwhile.

Nursery programs

The criteria applied when introducing equipment into the nursery is equally valid for computer programs. The educational value of both the content and the nature of learning needs to be considered. The merry tunes and colourful facade of some programs can reveal, on closer inspection, exercises that test rather than teach, with the computer replacing the textbook. Programs on number recognition can prove too difficult for children unable to count or recognise even limited numbers. Conversely, children who can recognise numbers may not be sufficiently challenged. At best, these programs serve to reinforce knowledge and accustom children to the keyboard.

More successful programs are open-ended and offer the potential for language development. When two or more children worked with an adult there was opportunity for naming, describing, classifying, predicting and memorising. Children of varying language abilities can use such programs; each child being successful and yet challenged. Computer activities that relate to children's everyday lives can be extended into other areas of the nursery, such as construction, paint or modelling. Equally, the program can be introduced to enhance a current topic.

Presentation

The same high standards of presentation that are required when choosing books and other material need to be applied to computer software. Computer graphics must be clear and easily interpreted. Often screens are crowded and coloured backgrounds can confuse young children. The content and graphics need to reflect current ideas on sex equality and multicultural education. Stereotypes of class and age should be avoided. The fonts should be in a suitably large and uncluttered style, encouraging easy recognition. Some 'Write your name' programs have a font size that is too small for practical purposes.

Co-ordination

Demands on a child's co-ordination should be realistic. The number and location of keys to be pressed need careful consideration if the child is to be encouraged to work independently. Children require sufficient time to respond to the program and the requirement of manipulative skills must be taken into account. In the most satisfactory programs, the child can control when the program moves forward.

Word processing

A standard infant word processing chip with large screen type, jumbo print and 'wysiwyg' (what you see is what you get) facility is useful for shared writing. Composing, the gathering and sorting of ideas, and transcribing, writing down in an appropriate format, can be demonstrated when the teacher acts as scribe. The child decides on a subject while the teacher interacts, helping the child to organise, extend and relate ideas.

This gives nursery children an excellent opportunity to practise storying skills that often lie undeveloped. It is important that young children, who have so much to say, become confident in their ability to initiate writing. The lack of something interesting and personal to express only becomes evident later when they can write but have nothing to say. Both content and form of writing need to be carefully nurtured from the beginning. Staff type as children talk.

Annabelle's subject was her baby: 'Byron my baby keeps wriggling like this and keeps scratching my face. He's a naughty boy. Byron cries all the time. Byron plays with my toys. Sometimes he's nice on a Tuesday or Wednesday, and then he gives me a cuddle.'

Forms and functions of print

The word processor can be used for any printing that is traditionally written by hand, although it is undesirable to exclude all handwriting. Children's own printed materials help their association of writing with book-print, as well as with environmental notices. Teachers assume they understand this link. Writing can be decontextualised and displayed on models or wherever relevent. Writing is passed to other staff to read aloud as children discover the public nature of writing as communication. A sense of audience soon develops.

Storying

Good starting points for word processing are a child's favourite rhyme, re-telling of stories, as well as children's own news and enthusiasms. Tales about the doll in the home corner or the further adventures of a well-loved puppet or soft toy, soon follow. These stories can be produced as individual or group books. Michael wanted to write about Ben: 'Ben runs away, and jumps over the gate. Do you know what he does next? He climbs over the gate and can't get in.'

Notices

Children not only dictate notices for the writing centre noticeboard, but also attach them to models, explaining how they were made. Signs for the home corner can be printed: 'Kim will cut your hair. Please wait here.' Letters can be written and 'posted' to children in another class to demonstrate the function of print as communication. The purpose of literacy for young children is usually immediate and self-initiated: composing inserts for cards to greet new siblings, parents in hospital or grandparents on their birthday. Typed captions accompany our photograph album of shared nursery experience, the daily routine, special events and visitors.

To aid memory and inform

Children can describe how a tower was constructed, what happened to certain objects in the water tray and record baking. Gemma explained: 'My mummy makes cream cakes with me. Well, you roll the pastry and then you put the cream on with a spoon, and you have to put them in the oven. Then we eat them up.'

Staff, of course, find word processing useful for parent notices.

Oral drafting

An adult reading screen type and print out enables young children to associate talking with typing. The situation may offer opportunities for oral drafting: asking children to extend their ideas 'Tell me more about ...', or encouraging them to develop a promising storyline. Children soon realise how easy it is to alter words.

The role of the adult may solely be to sustain and encourage a child's efforts. For very young children, it is the process that offers the educational experience: initiating topic, watching the use of the keyboard and reading subsequent screen type and print out, on which they may well choose to draw or make marks. Where several children contribute to group stories, discussion of what is to be included makes the drafting process explicit.

Adult as model

While staff, parents and anyone willing to press down a key, typed children's words, the children were spectating. They observed how adults searched for the correct key and how the key was pressed; the use of space bar and shift key. They watched the left to right direction of print, and compared the slowness of writing with the speed of speech. The drafting process was made explicit through discussion and the rearranging of text.

But they can't write!

Just as children imitate adult reading and writing behaviour, so they begin to imitate word processing behaviour. Given the opportunity to use the keyboard under supervision, children's understanding develops in a similar pattern to early writing.

1 **Exploration** Keys were pressed and children were thrilled to watch rows of letters appear and then disappear, as they learned to use the delete key. For many children this was sufficient in itself, enhanced by the thrill of printing their letters. Some children attributed these letters with meaning: 'That says your name'.

2 **Identifying letters** Just as children seek to identify and write their name by hand, so they want to know which keys make their name. Children readily recognise the upper case keyboard and the fact that the lower case may appear is accepted. Indeed, it may help children to match upper case and lower case letters. Any discrepancy can be discussed. At this stage children appreciate the importance of pressing the key firmly, but lightly, to only type one letter. This makes considerable demands on their manipulative skill but they are motivated to succeed. Name cards, including their typed name, are useful.

3 **A child produces her name** This may vary if a similar key to one in her name has been pressed, H instead of N, or the sequencing of letters in her name is not yet established. This usually indicates that the child is using visual discrimination rather than memory. Once a child can type her name, she soon learns to type the name of other family members, pets and classmates.

Emma

Emma (4 years 6 months) always enjoyed having her stories and songs written down. One day she declared, 'I'm going to do it!' Slowly and deliberately, she told her story at writing pace, pressing a key with each word or syllable she said. Sometimes she remained silent or repeated words while she pressed more keys, recognising that some words take longer to write. She searched the keyboard for a particular letter, and occasionally she made 'mistakes' and would delete and replace single letters.

While Emma wrote her story on the word processor, I wrote down the story she told on paper! Emma's imitation of computer literacy behaviour showed how much she knew about composing stories, the slow pace of writing, and the use of the keyboard.

Concept keyboard

The concept keyboard offers potential to develop whole word recognition. The overlay can consist of words and rebus technique, placing a picture instead of a word. Initially, overlays can be made with pictures from catalogues or in 3D, using different materials and actual objects. Children press the object and the appropriate word appears on screen.

Alternatives offer children opportunities to discuss and choose. One overlay I made, featured a fur fabric rabbit. The word 'likes' was followed by a choice of pictures, including cake, apple, banana and a mirror where the child's reflection appeared for the response 'me'.

Another idea is to use children's own photographs, possibly the sample roll left by the school photographer. On pressing the photograph, the child's name appears on the screen. The large concept keyboard provides sufficient space for the necessary size of writing and pictorial representation. Topics of general interest feature on overlays. One entitled 'Myself' has coloured squares corresponding to a variety of colours and rebus for eyes and hair. A child can successfully produce sentences with personal characteristics.

As children progress, overlays can be made for individuals featuring the first words with which they are familiar. It is possible to make one large complex word bank, but to present a child with a separate overlay containing only those words known to her. More words from the word bank can be written in as the child requires them. This provides material to suit individual needs.

Word processing with the concept keyboard can help whole word recognition, but offers only limited vocabulary. This activity does not address the purposeful use of print for an audience. Some ready-made concept keyboard programs claim to 'develop manipulative skills' or 'visual discrimination' but pay scant attention to what children are learning. Many nursery activities achieve these aims but also offer opportunities for spatial awareness, shape and representation.

Games can be devised for use on the concept keyboard. I made a 'Zoo Game' where after throwing a dice, a counter was moved. To receive instructions, the child pressed the square on which the counter landed: picnic here go back 1, or see an ice-cream van go forward 2. There was a basket of plastic animals beside the computer and instructions such as 'find a crocodile' were followed. Such games depend on an audit reading the screen for young children. This idea could be successfully used with readers in the infant school.

Educational value

Children learn computing by watching others and by using the keyboard. Nursery programs need to be sufficiently open-ended to enhance children's development, offering scope for a variety of teaching approaches, including problem solving and investigation. Programmers should consider more carefully the needs and capabilities of young children and offer opportunities for them to work together and share ideas.

Word processing with the adult acting as scribe, gives children the opportunity to develop story telling, as well as demonstrates the functions of print, making notices and books for others. With the adult acting as model, children learn the skills of the keyboard and appreciate the different modes of writing and speech.

Given the opportunity, children's computer literacy follows the stages of early writing with letter patterns at first random, but later developing into deliberately chosen letter strings. Word processing behaviour is evident in children through their use of the keyboard. Word processing does not diminish the importance of mark-making in the nursery but it does acknowledge the role of computer literacy in today's society.

Computers in the nursery must offer educational value. Use of word processing and computer programs must reflect the aims and objectives of good nursery practice, encouraging child-initiative, giving scope for individual development and adult interaction. Organisation of their use in the classroom needs to pay regard to social and language development. The computer tends to be 'teacher intensive' and staff need to ensure that their prolonged presence at the computer does not reduce the importance of other activities in the eyes of the children and should allocate their time accordingly. Use of the computer during the day can vary from word processing, demanding an adult presence, to computer programs that children can often tackle unassisted in pairs. Both NNEB and teacher training students are keen to assist, and the computer can also become a focus for parental involvement.

Rather than an isolated activity, subject to its own laws, computing needs to become an integral part of the on-going curriculum, true to the fundamental concepts of nursery education.

MICROS AND MATHS IN THE PRIMARY CLASSROOM

Ian Thompson *School of Education, University of Newcastle*

When microcomputers first arrived on the educational scene several years ago they were closely associated in many teachers' minds with mathematics. It was felt that you had to be mathematically inclined to be able to use them, and that their only use would be for the teaching of mathematics. Most of the earliest programs actually were mathematical in nature and were almost all of the structured reinforcement variety (a euphemism for 'drill and practice') testing either multiplication tables or the four basic arithmetical operations.

Since that time the CET, MEP, MESU, advisers and teacher educators around the country have attempted, and to a certain extent succeeded, in persuading teachers that microcomputers and associated items of software such as databases, simulations, adventure games and word-processors, have a great deal to contribute to the primary curriculum as a whole.

This article is an attempt to make a case for the use of the microcomputer in the teaching of primary mathematics, and will take the form of a consideration of some of the aims and objectives for the teaching of the subject as set out in HMI's recent document *Mathematics from 5 to 16*[1] along with suggestions of computer programs that could assist in the achievement of these particular aims and objectives. The software discussed will be limited, where possible, to cheap or freely-copiable programs. The paragraph headings are direct quotations from the section on aims and objectives included in the document.

'Performing Basic Operations'

HMI emphasise that even though the ability to perform the basic skills is important teachers need to ensure that these skills are not practised or tested out of context. An excellent program for providing children with the opportunity of practising the four rules of number in a stimulating context is 'Blocks,'[2] a 'Connect 4' type of game where children in teams of one or two compete against each other to gain possession of four squares in a line (horizontal, vertical or diagonal) on a numbered grid. The computer generates three numbers at random for each team in turn, and the children have to combine these three numbers using any mathematical operations they like in order to make their chosen number. The game generates a lot of excitement whilst at the same time obliging children to perform a great deal of mental arithmetic as they combine their numbers in order to make progress or to prevent their opponents from making progress. It could provide a focus for the introduction of brackets or simple powers to top juniors, but can be played successfully without this knowledge by much younger children.

'Working Cooperatively' and 'Ability to Communicate Mathematics'

Ever since the appearance of the Cockcroft Report in 1982 mathematical discussion has become an important aspect in the teaching and learning of mathematics at all levels. As children are to be assessed in their GCSE examination on their ability to discuss mathematical ideas it is important that children in primary schools are provided with the opportunity to talk about mathematics with their peers. Groupwork, which is more common in primary than in secondary school, is an obvious organisational structure to facilitate such discussion.

'Boiled Eggs,'[2] a program about the feasibility of using two different egg-timers to boil eggs for any given length of time, is flexible enough to allow different groups of two or three children to investigate different pairs of egg-timers. Not only does this program provide a focus for discussion within each small group but it also allows for each group to report its findings to the larger group so that a whole class discussion of the combined results can take place. Consideration of the combined data is more likely to result in children being able to see the underlying pattern – thereby putting them in a position to generalise their results.

'Understanding Basic Concepts'

It is generally accepted that the acquisition of a mathematical concept by children necessitates their experiencing a wide variety of situations in which the concept to be acquired is present in some form or other. Place value is a mathematical concept which, as most primary teachers know, many children have great difficulty in understanding. Practical work is essential if children are to come to terms with this difficult aspect of our number system, but use of the program 'Truck 10'[3] can provide children with further enjoyable experiences that can reinforce the concept of place value.

In the program a truck is loaded with a randomly selected number of barrels. After each load of ten is stacked in a triangular array the truck tips the barrels in columns of ten on the other side of the screen. At the end of the operation the child has to say how many lots of ten there are; how many there are left on the truck, and how many there are altogether. Computer feedback helps to reinforce the connections between these answers. The teacher can also control the range of the numbers selected.

'The Relationships between Concepts'

We read in paragraph 240 of the Cockcroft Report that:

> 'Conceptual structures are richly interconnecting bodies of knowledge . . . which . . . make up the substance of mathematical knowledge . . . (and) . . . underpin the performance of skills . . .'

It could be argued that the ability to make connections and perceive relationships between concepts is the hallmark of the able mathematician. Helping pupils make some of these necessary links is a difficult but essential task for the teacher.

The ability to interpret two-dimensional representations of three-dimensional objects can prove difficult for some children. The computer program 'Cubecount'[4] can help children to make this link. When asked to find the volume of, or count the number of cubes in, a three dimensional shape drawn on paper many children simply count the number of cubes they can see, and disregard the hidden ones. In 'Cubecount' a random collection of interlocking cubes appears on the left-hand side of the screen, and children are invited to count them. If a child makes an error the computer builds up the picture one row and one level at a time on the right-hand side of the screen thereby illustrating the hidden cubes before proceeding to cover them up. Although children could, and should, be given first-hand practical experience of making and dismantling three-dimensional shapes, it would be almost impossible to produce this dynamic two-dimensional effect without using a computer.

'Using Mathematics in Context'

An excellent example of a program which demands that mathematics be used throughout, and at all times in context, is 'Cars – Maths in Motion'.[5] This program simulates a Grand Prix race where teams of children prepare their cars for the big race at any of ten different tracks. In order to do this they have to measure the lengths of the straights on the circuit plan; find the angle of the bends; use percentages to find their safe speeds; read and interpret a weather report in order to decide on the type of tyres to fit; calculate the optimum amount of fuel needed, and interpret lap times given in decimals. All of this mathematics is used in a meaningful and enjoyable context, and the program has provided enough on-going topic work for a class of third year (Y5) junior children for a whole year.

'Ability to Estimate'

All teachers of mathematics would agree that estimation is a very necessary skill, but a cursory glance at both teacher-produced and commercial schemes of work would suggest that we actually only pay lip-service to this very important notion. It is difficult to find ideas in these schemes which would succeed in developing this skill effectively. The main type of activity usually involves asking the children to estimate before making a calculation or a measurement. But what children actually do is calculate or measure first, and then make the estimation afterwards. This is unfortunate since we are dealing with a skill of increasing importance in an age of calculator usage.

A simple, but useful, program which gives children practice at estimating the size of angles to the nearest ten degrees is 'Angles'.[6] Answers that are not considered accurate enough are dynamically illustrated by a rotating arm with ten degree sectors shaded in different colours to enable the child to improve her estimate next time. The frequency of practice and immediacy of positive (or at least non-negative) feedback would appear to give children a better feeling for angle measurement than any manner of teacher-directed activity. If this program, or others like it, were used before teaching children to use the notorious semi-circular protractor it could help prevent the common error of reading from the wrong scale.

'Ability to Approximate'

If estimation strategies are to be encouraged and developed then approximation techniques need to be understood, learned and practised. Research carried out for the Cockcroft Committee suggested that adults do not feel confident or at ease about giving approximate answers to questions. The 'hidden curriculum' of the mathematics classroom has taught them that answers to mathematical problems must at all times be exact.

Approximate answers to numerical calculations are the theme of 'Number Chaser',[7] a program with bright, colourful and noisy graphics. Children participate in a car race, and in order to make progress they have to select one number from a choice of four which lies nearest to the answer to a given multiplication sum. There are four different levels, and playing at the higher levels can provide a context for the discussion of strategies (a combination of rounding, multiplication by powers of ten and single-digit multiplication) for finding approximate answers mentally.

The following objectives are more concerned with the acquisition and development of problem-solving strategies than with the learning of skills or the understanding of concepts. A recurring theme throughout the HMI document is the emphasis on children finding their own way through problems using their own idiosyncratic methods, and working in a supportive situation that stimulates them to ask and attempt to answer their own questions.

'Trial and Error Methods'

Children, and adults too, often have the idea that trial and error methods are inferior problem solving strategies which have little or no place in mathematics. Primary school teachers on inservice courses have been known to apologise for using such methods to solve problems. Trial and error methods often enable problem-solvers to get involved with the problem and reach a clearer understanding of what the problem means before they proceed to use some more systematic method of solution. Sometimes they can prove to be useful strategies for finding a resolution to the actual problem itself. Polya whose

seminal book *How to Solve it*[8] was one of the earliest to address the issue of the teaching of problem solving heuristics, argued quite forcibly that we should actually teach guessing, and made the valid point that in mathematics and science the guess often precedes the proof.

In the 'Colouring Problem',[9] a computer version of the four-colour map problem, you have to colour a map of your choice in such a way that no two adjacent regions are the same colour. The cursor key is positioned over the region to be coloured, and, at the press of a key, one of six colours immediately fills the region selected. You are asked how many colours you think will be needed before you start, but the aim is to use as few different colours as possible. The program offers a great deal of opportunity for modification of solutions as colours can be erased and replaced quite simply and instantaneously.

'Simplifying Difficult Tasks' and 'Looking for Pattern'

Two very important mathematical problem solving strategies are specialising and generalising. The latter involves the search for a pattern which will enable you to predict not only the next instance but any and all instances. Specialising, on the other hand, is concerned with exploring special cases in order to achieve involvement with the problem and to develop a feeling for what is required. Consideration of a simplified version of the original problem often makes the search for pattern somewhat easier.

A standard investigation, which goes under various names in the literature, concerns a strange billiard table, say, 25 by 9 which is marked out in squares and has just four pockets at the corners. A ball is struck from the top left corner at an angle of 45 degrees to the edges of the table, and bounces off the cushions finally to land in one of the pockets. The problem is to find how many contacts were made with the cushion, and which pocket the ball will finally land in. The computer program 'Bounce'[2] simulates this problem but will allow the contruction of tables of any size before asking for your guess and then dynamically demonstrating the cushion contacts. The computer does the spadework and leaves you to collect the data, tabulate the information, search for patterns and make and test conjectures.

'Making and Testing Hypotheses'

In some primary classrooms children, when provided with a suitable stimulus or starting point rich in mathematical potential, have developed enough confidence to be able to ask and formulate their own mathematical questions. This situation often produces a higher motivational level and a more determined attempt on behalf of the problem posers to pursue the problems to their conclusion.

In order to use computers in this way what is needed is more open-ended, non-directive, 'toolbox' or utility software. There are few programs of this nature currently available that are suitable for primary school children, but 'Longsums'[10] is an exception. All this program does is calculate. However, the advantage it has over a calculator is that it will give answers of any size without resorting to the more complicated standard form notation, and without being restricted by the limitations of an eight-digit display. This allows the multiplication of large numbers and the continuation and exploration of interesting patterns such as $111 \times 111 = 12321$, $1111 \times 1111 = 1234321$, etc. Other potential investigations include the exploration of the decimal equivalents of fractions (the seventeenths are particularly interesting), and can provide a context for the early introduction of recurring decimals to top juniors (Y6).

This article has attempted to argue that there is now a wide range of educationally sound computer software suitable for the teaching and learning of mathematics in the junior school, and that the use of this material could well assist in the achievement of many of the objectives for the teaching of mathematics set out in *Mathematics from 5 to 16*. Not only should the use of such software enhance the teaching of mathematics, but should make the learning of the subject a much more enjoyable process – thereby achieving the final objective listed in *Mathematics from 5 to 16*, namely, 'A Positive Attitude to Mathematics'.

References

1 DES, (1985) *Mathematics from 5 to 16*. London, HMSO.

2 'Blocks', 'Boiled Eggs' and 'Bounce' from 'Primary Maths and Micros' MEP INSET Pack. Available from LEA Maths Advisers.

3 'Truck 10' is a Blue File program available free of charge from any SEMERC.

4 'Cubecount' is on 'Educational 1' from Golem Ltd, 77 Qualitas, Bracknell, Berks RG12 4QG.

5 'Cars – Maths in Motion' from Cambridge Software House, Town Hall, St Ives, Cambs.

6 'Angles' is on 'Maths Practice in the Classroom' from Capital Media, c/o ILECC, John Ruskin St, London SE5 3BE.

7 'Number Chaser' from ASK, London House, 68 Upper Richmond St, London SW15 2RP.

8 Polya G. (1945) *How to Solve it*', Princeton Press: New Jersey.

9 'Colouring Problem' is on 'Maths with a Story – Volume 1', from BBC Publications, 35 Marylebone High St, London W1M 4AA.

10 'Longsums' on 'Maths with a Micro' from RLDU, Bishop Rd, Bishopston, Bristol BS7 8LS.

'MOVE OVER MATHS': using a computer in topic

Lez Smart   *Liberty Middle School, Merton*

When computers were first introduced into schools one of the immediate concerns was, 'Who is going to be responsible for 'it'?' In the era of falling rolls and therefore reduced availability of scale points it was often found necessary to add the responsibility for 'it' to an already existing post of responsibility. This was particulary true in primary and middle schools. Sometimes it was added to the AVA portfolio, sometimes it was added to the load of 'the jack of all trades' deputy head, while in other cases the head accepted the responsibility. However, I would suggest that any survey conducted into this allocation of responsibility for the computer would find that in most cases it was linked to the post of responsibility given to mathematics.

This was, at least unfortunate, and often disastrous for the way the computer was perceived by the children and the rest of the staff, for such perceptions have adversely affected the uses it has been put to. To emphasise the point, I have yet to hear of responsibility for the computer being held by the person holding the post of responsibility for language policy or English. This legacy of computers being tied to mathematics, both physically and in our own thinking, symbolically, has proved to be restrictive.

In this article, I attempt to outline how the computer was used as part of an environmental studies/science topic and to show how the initial, and in retrospect, narrow role envisaged for the computer came to assume a much broader dimension and to make a much greater contribution to the children's learning process.

A team of three staff working in the second year (10-11 year olds) (Y6) of our 9-13 Middle School, in an industrial suburb on the edge of London, decided to give over the main part of the Autumn term to a study of 'The Weather'. The planning had involved the drawing up of a flow diagram that took the children into all the traditional curriculum areas. However one of our major aims was to attempt to bring the child to a realisation that the weather they experienced was not arbitrary but was open to rational explanation. This fitted into our overall aim of seeing education as a process whereby the children are helped to understand and make sense of their world and their experience of it. The collection and collation of information on major variables such as the temperature, the wind direction and speed, the presence of cloud and its type would, we hoped, provide the basis for some hypothesis formation and testing as the work developed. We sought to show that the information collected could be presented in a variety of ways ie tables, graphs, diagrams. We also intended to put our readings onto a database[1] programme we had for our BBC microcomputer[2]. We intended that the putting in and taking out of the information would increase the 'computer literacy' of our pupils. We also envisaged being able to call up particular information as required at a speed which would demonstrate the use of the computer for data handling.

Our previous use of the computer had been confined to commercially produced material and although 'interesting' we had reservations about its value of two major grounds. Firstly, some of the programmes did little that could not be achieved by the using of material traditionally used eg clock faces with movable hands, Dienes blocks etc. A more serious criticism however was that while several of the simulation/game programmes had value they had usually to be used in isolation from the main theme/topic of the class's work. At the planning stage, therefore, although impressed with the technology, we were rather sceptical of the contribution of the computer to our mainstream programmes of learning.

Over the Autumn term the children developed their power of observation and recorded their findings and readings in a variety of ways. One of these was the entry into the database programme of the weekly reading for temperature, wind direction, wind force, rainfall.[3] Our initial aims for the computer were being realised in that the children were becoming quite adept at entering and editing their readings, and there were several occasions when the speed with which we could extract information about one aspect or one particular day was demonstrably faster than checking the graphs, charts and diagrams.

However it was towards the final phase of the topic that we realised our aims for the computer had been set much too low. We had intended that, as the work developed, the children would begin to observe similarities in their observations and readings and from these pose hypotheses which they could attempt to test. A simple example would be to see if there was a correlation between warm days and wind direction, or rain and type of cloud. Obviously these questions could be answered by working through the graphs and charts, but it was at this stage that we began to realise the computer might have a greater contribution to make.

Working in pairs and small groups the children began to work out how to extract the information they had previously put in. Slowly at first, but with increasing dexterity they worked out that you could have the information back in any form you wanted and, eventually, in the form that suited your purpose best. Although initially the various commands had been demonstrated to the children this decision-making about 'what' information you wanted, and (just as important) what you didn't want, and how you wanted it presented, was worked out within each group with no, or with minimal, intervention by the teacher. There were many examples of the type of discussion that Barnes[4] illustrated as being so valuable, as the children worked out their own thoughts and strategies by 'bouncing' their ideas off each other. Many of the tasks set originated with the teacher eg 'Is there any pattern that you can see between when it rains and where the wind is coming from' or 'Where would you expect the wind to be coming from on the coldest days? – and were you right?'

However as confidence grew, the children were encouraged to ask their own questions or check their own statements out eg 'It always rains on games afternoons' or 'I wonder who had the best weather on their birthday?' (and did 'best' mean 'warmest' or 'not wet' or what?)

Once the question had been agreed upon, the group had then to work out how to extract the information they wanted. Many times the phrase 'you can't say that, *it* won't understand you, you've got to ask *it* in computer language' was heard. Eventually, a print-out would be obtained and pored over. Often it was scrapped or someone realised that if they had asked *it* to do 'this' (for example SORT all the wind directions so that all the N came together etc) it would be easier to work out what they wanted to find out. The 'product' of the task was often a graph or a Venn Diagram or a brief report to the class on their findings and the way they had arrived at them.

What we began to find, and which we thought very encouraging was that two further developments were occurring. Firstly, the results of one task were forming the basis for another new one, sometimes a supplementary one but also at times quite independent. For example, one child noticed that the children whose birthdays were in October did not always have better (in this case, warmer) weather than those with birthdays in November. This led to an hypothesis (and I think it deserves to be called this) that November must be colder than October because it was 'more into Winter'. Using the computer he was able to test this out and indeed develop it, to see if December was colder than November, using the same criteria.

The second development which occurred was when we began to attempt to predict the weather. What kind of day could one expect if the wind direction was x, the speed y and the cloud cover z? With ease we were now able to see what had happened the last time, or the last 10 times, this combination had occurred. Did this mean that what happened then (rain and sunny spells) would happen today or were there other variables at play?

There are many other examples, but from these it is possible to make several observations on the contribution of the computer to our topic.

At a fundamental level the use of the database had overcome our earlier concern that computer work was too 'once removed' from the unified curriculum we were working towards. It had become a key part of it and was used along with the reference books, the videos of the weather forecasts, the thermometers, rain gauges etc – that is, when it was the most appropriate piece of equipment to use.

However, when we met to review and reflect on this topic we realised that its contribution had been much greater than that of merely another tool. We would make two major claims for the computer in a topic of this or similar nature. These are obviously inter-related but can be separated. Firstly the computer acted as a catalyst for the children's thinking about the weather and its component parts. It acted as a central point for discussions, many of them of a problem-solving (eg what command to use, and in what order) or hypothesis testing (eg if the wind is from the north it will snow) nature.

Secondly, and finally, we would argue that it encouraged higher level thinking. This is a large claim and is one that is not made lightly. But the computer, by its ability and speed to respond to questions and present information in the desired way, removed the 'chore element' from many of the tasks either set by ourselves or the children. It became possible for these 10–11 year olds to decide on a question, hypothesise about what the answer might be, work out a strategy and have the results within a reasonable, that is 'un-daunting' period of time. We believe this actively encouraged the children to pose more questions and form more hypotheses than they would otherwise have done. In mathematics I think people talk about using the machine to 'number crunch', that is do the manual exercises that can be so laborious and time-consuming. Some will argue that the children should be made to compile their supporting data in the traditional way. However we would argue that this 'if it's going to do you good it's got to hurt' approach is counter productive in that, knowing they will be asked to support what they say, some children will refrain from suggesting it in the first place.

One concluding comment on an area touched upon but not developed here is the amount and quality of discussion that took place in the small groups clustered around the keyboard. There is no space to expand upon this here, other than to suggest that colleagues in schools doing similar work should listen in to these discussions – they are likely to be pleasantly surprised! The discussions illustrated Barnes'[4] hypothesis that children use 'exploratory language' to sort out their ideas. It is possible that they are more likely to do this in small peer groups than in whole class discussion with the teacher. The computer obviously has a contribution to make to mathematics teaching but we think it has a lot more to offer right across the curriculum. As more and more colleagues realise this perhaps the cry will be heard 'Move over maths – if only a little!'

References

[1] We used QUEST produced by A.C.U.B.E.
[2] The microcomputer referred to is a standard BBC (32k) model connected to a Cumana Disk Drive, a Cub Monitor and a Walters Printer.
[3] The field names we set up were day, date, month, temperature, wind direction, wind force, rainfall, description. Cloud cover and cloud type were added at a later date.
[4] Barnes D. (1976) *From Communication To Curriculum*, Penguin.

ADVISORY OR SUPPORT TEACHERS IN PRIMARY EDUCATION?

Chris Jones   *ESG Primary Science and Technology Support Teacher, West Midlands*

Brenda Lofthouse's article[1] in *Education 3-13*, Volume 15, Number 3, challenges the value of the Primary Science and Technology ESG (Education Support Grant) work. During the past four terms I have been a member of an ESG-funded support team and my own experiences contradict much of what Brenda Lofthouse describes.

In planning their overall support for primary science and technology, my employing authority has developed a fully integrated approach, linking the ESG-funded activities within the existing Curriculum Support Team. No 'new structure' has been established and I feel my own authority, and others, are well prepared for the ESG support.

The project team consists of three experienced 'support' teachers. The role of the team is wide and varied: 'change agents'; 'catalysts'; 'facilitators'; 'exemplars of good practice'; 'encouragers'; 'enthusiasts' and 'builders'. Team members were selected on the basis of the following criteria: they are above average classroom practitioners; have their ability to influence colleagues; they have knowledge and experience of teaching in more than one school; they have a 'good' INSET attendance record; have worked with adults and appreciate the fact that working in this way requires different skills to 'normal' teaching; they are adaptable; they demonstrate initiative, creativity and imagination; and have sufficient expertise and experience to earn respect, and be respected, in the role of support teacher.

The general aim of the ESG Project is to raise the level of teachers' awareness, confidence and competence in the teaching and learning of primary science and technology, so that staff may develop their own thinking and understanding. As part of this strategy, the team attempts to remove the 'mystique' from science and technology by showing that practical, investigative and

problematic science and technology is fun for both teacher and children. Above all, the project team is charged with ensuring that science and technology becomes a permanent and integral part of the broad and balanced primary curriculum.

The following paragraphs outline how one project team of West Midlands support teachers implement the above aims. It is not an easy task.

When working with teachers, either in school or during centre-based practical workshops, the support team does not merely hand the 'Curriculum Project' to them as 'products'. Teachers, whether they are classteachers, co-ordinators or headteachers, are closely involved in the processes of review, development and implementation, and are encouraged to start at their own base line, and move at their own pace, in response to what they see to be their needs, and their pupils' needs. The team seeks to draw out, and where necessary, improve, what is there, by actively involving teachers in thinking (or re-thinking) what they 'do' rather than try to 'advise' them about new practices. Curriculum and staff development involve changing attitudes and practices of individual teachers within the context of the whole organisation of the school. The effectiveness of any such change depends upon staff concerned recognising the need for change; being aware of alternatives; and being confident in their relationships. With this in mind, the project team is concerned with a 'whole school approach' to curriculum and staff development, involving all the staff and, where possible, parents and governors. The whole purpose of the team's involvement is to develop a climate of thought, learning, cooperation and confidence throughout the school, not simply in isolated pockets. The process of development and growth, and possibly long term change, will only be effective if the staff are fully committed and willing to participate in what is considered to be a legitimate exercise, and if the support team are seen to be fully informed of current practice and effectively involved with colleagues in schools. The project team works 'to do things with' individuals and staff, not 'to them'.

In order to meet the needs of staff, and schools, the ESG Project Team offers many strategies of support; they fall into three broad categories: school-based support; centre-based support; and 'other types' of support.

A high proportion of ESG time is spent in schools, supporting teachers in the promotion of primary science and technology. A total of three days a week is spent in this way. Involvement of the Project Team in schools follows certain procedures: invitations and requests from schools are directed, in writing, to either the Head of the Curriculum Support Team, who is also the Primary Inspector, and/or the Inspector for Science and Technology. Following the request for an involvement, either one or both of the inspectors contacts the school, or a member of the Project Team, to discuss a possible involvement. The category of support available to school is determined via discussion and negotiation.

There are many categories of school-based support: Category 'A' Schools receive a termly commitment of the equivalent of one day per week, or in some cases half-a-day per week, from the project team, and an input of at least one term, possibly two, at this level of support, is anticipated; schools which have been within Category 'A', but not longer have a weekly commitment, are described as Category 'B'. In this instance, a formal programme of follow up support is agreed upon between the staff, usually all, and the team within the procedures already established. Types of follow-up which may be offered are many: after the initial Category 'A' support, it may be appropriate for the team to assist in establishing a framework for dissemination through lower or upper school, or throughout the school; ensuring that all staff are fully aware of the opportunity to join working parties to develop materials and exchange ideas; set up 'cluster' meetings, to review long term aims; and ensure contacts and limited support are maintained. Schools receiving support, other than a weekly commitment, are classified as Category 'C'. Category 'D' schools are those requesting school-based support through their GRIST programmes.

Sixty percent of the project team members' time is spent working in Category 'A' schools. Schools are selected as Category 'A' schools depending on a number of criteria: staff commitment to staff and curriculum development; sci-

ence and techology identified as a GRIST priority; the machinery, which will enable development to take place, is present within the school's management structure; staff have attended recent INSET programmes with regards to science and technology; the school has a coordinator for science and technology; the school has participated in, and entered exhibits for, the Walsall Science and Technology Fair.

Should a school feel school-based support is appropriate/needed, or any other type of support, the headteacher is encouraged to send a 'request', in writing, to either of the two inspectors directly involved in the coordination of the team. Following that initial request, one of the inspectors visits the school to discuss the request further, and a decision is made as to the appropriate category of support to be made available to the school. No school is turned away completely. Schools not receiving Category 'A' support are offered an alternative input. If a school is identified as a Category 'A' school, the following term, there follows a period of discussion initially with the headteacher and coordinator, and then extends to include all the staff. This allows the team to communicate the purposes of the project, identify the role of the support teacher, the intentions of the ESG team, and the part to be played by the school and staff.

During this early period of discussion, the team begin to assess the present situation in the school, and identify the needs of the staff: have there been any recent curriculum review and development exercises which have had a particular bearing upon the science and technology curriculum; the present 'state of play' with regards present science/technology policy/practice; effectiveness of present policy; summaries of the main conclusions and recommendations for review, developmental and implementation work; what are the various in-service needs of the staff; how are these needs to be met; how are the staff going to monitor what is happening during the involvement; how will staff use to assess the effectiveness of the involvement; what criteria will staff use to assess the effectiveness of the involvement; when will the staff assess the effectiveness of the involvement.

There now follows a period of negotiation with the headteacher, coordinator and classteacher, to identify a 'programme', a 'way forward, that encompasses the following: the actual needs of the staff and curriculum, rather than the headteachers's perceived needs, which are not necessarily the same, and ways that they can be met; identify objectives and methods of working within the school and classes; and formulate methods of assessment and evaluation.

The purposes of the project are conveyed to all the staff and they are asked to identify the 'issues' relating to the science and technology curriculum, or broader issues they would like to see included in the review, development and implementation. To enable them to do this, each member of staff is asked to complete a questionnaire. Section 1 asks each individual member of staff to identify which of the following they would like to see reviewed and developed: what is science and technology and how does it relate to primary children; what processes, skills, attitudes and concepts should be developed through the approach; problem solving as an approach; questions and problems as starting points for investigations; experiences; topic planning; lesson planning; classroom organisation and management; resources; assessment, recording; progression and continuity; role of the classteacher, headteacher and coordinator; evaluation of the policy; towards a policy. Section 2 asks each member of staff to select six issues, Identified in Section 1, and Including any issues identified themselves, but not included in the original list, which they feel would benefit from review; the staff are then asked to prioritise these six issues in rank order. Section 3 asks each member of staff to select from the areas of experience what they feel they would benefit from a practical workshop session, or series of sessions. The areas of experience suggested include: Ourselves; Animals and Plants; Environment and Weather; Materials; Structures; Energy and Control.

The returns are then analysed by the team member(s), coordinator and headteacher. In this way the needs of the staff are identified and a way to meet these needs can be planned. Alongside this negotiation and planning, which involves the whole staff, is the negotiation and planning involving the classteachers whom the project team is going to work alongside.

Following the three or four weeks of discussion, negotiation and planning, a 'contract' is jointly drawn up which considers the needs of the school as well as the support offered.

Much of the work in schools is classroom-based with team members directly involved in teaching children. Work in the classroom, when both the classteacher and the support teacher(s) are present, is collaborative. Usually, though not always, a single group of children are involved with a scientific/technological element of the topic/theme/project, while the remaining groups tackle other 'topic-related' work. This element is important in order to promote the professional development of the classteacher, and unless teachers are able to develop and extend new teaching strategies there will be no 'long term' professional and curriculum development.

The preparation of work and the selection topic/theme/project is a joint activity with the classteacher. Time is arranged so that the classteacher and team members, or a team member, can be together for joint preparation/review/follow up/evaluation.

Continuous evaluation is important in that, if necessary, the 'contract' can be amended, objectives and/or ways of working changed, etc. Very occasionally there is a need to readjust the initial contract, while there is still time available in school. At the conclusion of the Category 'A' Support, there is a series of further negotiation and planning sessions to identify which objectives have (have not) been achieved and 'the where next'? Part of the Category 'B' support includes follow up visits from the team to maintain contact, offer support and 'gently' remind staff of their good intentions. The staff are asked to complete a questionnaire to assess the involvement and the returns are analysed to help in the planning of future support. Eight weeks after the Category 'A' involvement is completed, the headteacher is also asked to complete a questionnaire, requesting an evaluation of the involvement, a report on progress and recent developments, and outlining the school's 'way forward'. Using this strategy, the ESG Support Team are accountable to the schools and, as important, the schools are, some ways, accountable to the ESG team.

Schools receiving input, but not in the form of either a Category 'A' or 'B' involvement, receive a less intensive form of support.

Running alongside the school-based support, the ESG team uses centre-based inservice workshops and courses, as an additional part of the support strategy, which are well attended. In some cases supply cover is provided to enable teachers and headteachers to attend during the school day.

The courses provided differ in audience, content and timing. All courses are open to headteachers, and, in future, courses will be provided specifically addressed to headteachers. The crucial role of the headteacher is acknowledged.

Courses are being provided specifically concerned with the younger child. Discussions with nursery and infant teachers reveal a need for many more courses which cater for the specific needs of the teacher of young children.

Since teachers frequently express lack of awareness, confidence and knowledge in physical science topics, such as 'energy' and 'forces', the majority of workshop topics have related to these areas. Problem solving/'Designing and Making'/technology courses have been appropriate for the introduction of physical science concepts in a non-threatening way.

The longer courses for coordinators tackle the difficult issues of identifying and meeting staff needs, the National Curriculum and assessment and recording. Methods of liaison to ensure continuity of science and technology education is considered.

Other forms of support are being implemented, alongside school and centre-based work: the project team is actively promoting the Walsall Science and Technology Fair, in conjunction with the TVEI Project; working with cluster groups of schools in order to examine the problems associated with transition from primary to secondary with particular reference to a continuity of provision in science and technology; development, in conjunction with teachers, of a range of appropriate resource material; the production of a set of documents (Health and Safety in Science and Technology in the Primary School; Classroom Organisation and Management; Problem Solving; Good Practice in Science and Technology; Talking Technology); the production, over three years, of a set of guidelines for the teaching of science and technology as part of the Primary Curriculum. In addition, the team is actively involved in linking with other ESG project teams.

The activities of the ESG support team are coordinated within the work of the longer-established Curriculum Support Team, by the inspector with responsibility for that team, in consultation with the Inspector for Science and Technology.

The aims and objectives, methods of working, school-based involvements, centre-based support, other forms of support, documentation, records, etc. are monitored in a number of ways, at a number of different levels: bi-weekly steering group meetings; observation of the team's work by inspectors; regular planning and evaluation meetings involving team members and teachers; feedback from pastoral inspectors; documentation; questionnaires; external evaluation.

The work of the project team in schools is monitored and its effectiveness evaluated by: the specification of clear initial objectives to be achieved and the close monitoring of outcomes; the statement, or 'contract' jointly made, between participating schools and the team of the expected outcomes from the involvement and the assessment of the actual degree of attain-

ment of these expectations; and the response of classteachers, the coordinator and headteacher by way of informal discussion and questionnaire returns.

After only four terms of the project, there is very little evidence on which to base predictions about long term changes. However, in the short term, an increasing number of children have been involved in practical, investigative science and technology. Support in the classroom has enabled children to undertake purposeful, practical activities within the framework of the children's own experience. Teachers have seen this as a more effective way of communicating the nature of primary science and technology than the lecture or seminar, conducted away from the classroom, in the absence of children, helping them to overcome their anxieties about the organisational and pedagogical issues. Entire teaching staffs are considering developments in science and technology in their school.

Science and Technology should not be a discrete addition to the primary curriculum, but should be an integral part of it. Primary science and technology can influence the development of skills, attitudes and concepts in other areas of the curriculum in two main ways. The approach can provide a relevant and practical opportunity for the application of learning developed in many other subjects. In this respect, primary science and technology has a supportive role within the curriculum. It can also stimulate new learning as children, involved in investigations and problem solving, research into possible solutions. In this way, primary science and technology has an initiating role.

LEAs should consider providing support for primary science and technology in the context of 'support' for the development of the whole curriculum.

The scale of the task is very great. In some schools considerable changes are needed in classroom practice to enable the sound development of primary science and technology. In my own LEA, it was recognised from the outset that it would be impossible to involve all schools during a three-year project. The DES/WO statement of policy, '5–16', recognises the need for INSET for teachers and it seems likely that the approaches developed in the ESG project will be particularly effective.

In the future, it will be important for strategies of school-based and centre-based support to be made available after 1989 (or 1988, depending on the LEA's commencement date) for those who identify the need support, or whose need is identified, but have not been able to receive it by that time. Other schools will need further support in order to sustain and develop the work promoted by ESG. I am aware that there are moves to extend the three-year ESG support, and I personally feel that this would be a more positive approach, in contrast to the creation of an 'advisory/inspectoral level.

When the ESG team members have worked in classrooms, reception by teachers has usually been positive. Few teachers have had experience of receiving this kind of support and some have been anxious about working with an 'expert'. Worries, I believe, have been short-lived. The acceptability of the support team has in-creased because they are seen as 'helpers', 'supporters', not 'advisors', 'inspectors' or 'evaluators'.

The Curriculum Support Team, within my own authority, together with the other support agencies, is sufficiently developed to enhance curriculum development of primary schools on a long term basis and I would propose that other LEAs create, extend and develop curriculum support strategies, and not establish an advisory/inspectoral level, between the schools and the present general inspectors. The key to professional and curriculum development lies in the wording, curriculum 'supporters', not 'advisers'.

Reference

[1] Lofthouse's article argued that advisory teachers in Science and Technology had difficulty in being effective, and it would be better to establish *curriculum advisory inspectors* with the status needed to influence practice in schools.

SUPPORTING SCIENCE: reflections of an advisory teacher

Max de Bóo   *formerly Haringey LEA*

Becoming an ESG Advisory teacher for Primary Science in September 1985 was difficult. There were few precedents and even fewer records of school-based support to provide me with useful guidelines. Until then, most support teachers in school had focused their attention directly on the children – helping those with language or other learning difficulties. Our LEA focus was to be the teachers and although this would obviously mean working with the children too, the aim was to improve the quality and quantity of science *teaching*. In many cases this meant trying to change teachers' attitudes towards science and the practice of it in their classrooms; and with just three years in which to do this, it felt like jumping into the deep end knowing only that the water was not ice-cold!

I was confident about what *I* meant by good primary science practice but less sure as to how to match my support to the needs of the teachers. I believed it was essential to adopt an approach of 'teacher-centred learning'. This meant being aware of the science background of the teachers, their feelings about the subject and confidence in teaching it, as well as showing respect for their expertise and experience in teaching in general. This made planning difficult. Just as any primary class teacher, I could plan and resource my support but must remain flexible and open-minded enough to modify my plans according to the situation in the classroom.

To help me to evaluate my own effectiveness I began to monitor the kinds of support I gave in school, whether asked for by the teacher or offered when appropriate. Over the months that followed a pattern began to emerge showing the variety of support given, varying from practical help to encouraging classroom research. It was then that I tried to isolate those aspects which seemed to signify a real change in the teaching of science. I tried to be scrupulously honest with my own, but nevertheless very subjective, records. I

was looking for an 'increase' in certain activities and that meant I could *not* record an increase where it was plain that the teacher already used a practical and purposeful approach to science. Thus the results tried to show the effect the school-based support might be having rather than simply recording what the teachers might be doing already. The support was classified into four main areas: information; classroom support; personal support; and changes observed.

Most support was asked for at the basic level. Teachers, and the school as a corporate body, needed information and practical ideas. Questions such as . . . 'Have you any ideas for investigations into "Air" for middle infants (Y1)?'; 'How deep should the water be for the tadpole tank?'; 'Can you recommend some software to expand our project on "Growth"?'; 'Which published scheme will give most help to us as nursery teachers?'. Experience meant that I could give immediate responses to these questions or soon afterwards. The questions are not new but 'being there' or accessible kept up the momentum of the science programme.

The next grouping represented the type of teaching support given in the classroom. This fell into four categories: teaching demonstrations, general teaching while the classteacher worked with a group on the science investigations, team-teaching, and assisting in a debate or dramatisation of a science/moral issue. The teachers showed a preference for team-teaching. The drawback here is that time has to be found to share and discuss the developments later (not always possible). Increasingly, the teachers began to value the opportunity to observe and discuss the ESG teacher's approach and questionning technique or a colleague's. Moral issues on the use of science were rarely discussed with the class.

The third grouping centred around personal support, increasing teachers' confidence in themselves and their science teaching, liaison, and presentation and persuasion in meetings with staff, parents and Governing bodies. There was a sense of being a personal ambassador for science and people would respond accordingly. This was a delicate area, requiring sensitivity and finesse. As teachers realised they were not being judged, rather respected for their professionalism, they responded with trust, open-mindedness and positive support for the science programme.

The final grouping represented the ways I saw changes occuring in the approach that individual teachers used in their science teaching. The results showed a slow start, an acceleration of change and a levelling off. They also showed an irregular pattern of change. I had expected to see an improvement in classroom investigative work, whereas what I actually observed was an improved technique in the use of open-ended questions (ie. questions such as 'What colour is the grass?' . . . expectation 'green' . . . changing to 'What colours do you think we will find on the plants in the school field?'). The results also indicated that as time went on, teachers were readier to share their ideas with me and in particular to reflect on their primary science work in an open and self-critical way, perhaps an indication of a growing confidence in themselves. What was valuable was that this system of recording support enabled me to modify my own performance as a source of information, improved classroom support techniques, gave me heightened awareness of personal support strategies and a clearer assessment of individual changes.

It was also necessary to look at schools as a whole. Some research has shown that effective change in a school is best achieved when the school operates as an entire unit and all the staff are involved in and committed to the change. My own LEA's submission to the DES had emphasised this and whole school staffs were working with the science initiative, showing enthusiasm and commitment. It was therefore possible to monitor change in the school as a whole. To do this I used the criteria devised by Joy Wilson (with the IPSE team), *Initiatives in Primary Science Evaluation,* and converted it, with amendments and additions, into a checklist. I had reservations about the checklist but did not want to spend time 're-inventing the wheel'. The resulting checklists are shown and by using a point score as indicated I was able to see patterns across a group of schools. I used the Masterfile program to record the results and made the data non-identifiable to preserve confidentiality. In many ways the results were not surprising, con-

firming as they did the results of previous studies (eg. the APU tests) but that gave me the confidence that my data was reasonably objective and also forced me into the realisation that if things had not changed significantly, then I must modify my approach to the school and individual teachers still further.

Classroom Evaluation

1. Is there purposeful activity within the framework of the child's experience? Are the children developing attitudes of curiosity, perseverance and self-discipline?
2. Are the children discussing work (talking to learn), listening/co-operating, communicating findings and procedures? Are the children developing attitudes of self-criticism, open-mindedness?
3. Is there genuine investigational work going on? Is it stimulated by the children's own interests?
4. Do the children try to guess, suggest why, try things out? Are the children using an approach that will lead to skills of observing, classifying, predicting, communicating, measuring?
5. Do the children devise their own experiments? Do they make fair tests?
6. Do the children repeat tests, check surprising results?
7. Do the children extend their work as a result of their findings? Apply their learning?

Classroom

It appeared that whilst a lot of purposeful investigations were being carried out in the classroom they were largely inspired by the teachers or planned by them. Less freedom was given to the children to initiate or devise their own tests. Children were not always being encouraged to repeat tests or suggest hypotheses to account for surprising results. Significantly, children were not being asked to extend or apply their learning, whether in science investigations or in other areas of the curriculum.

When I followed this up I discovered in discussion with the teachers that some of them found it difficult to actually 'isolate' and 'identify' the science (idea or concept) in an investigation. Without that, they could not begin to suggest ways of extending or applying the science. I consequently made the encouragement of this 'identification and application of science' as one of my main objectives, both in centre-based courses and in

Checklist 1. Classroom evaluation

	1	2	3	4	5	6	7	8	9	10	11	12	13	14	15
1. Purposeful activity . . . curiosity, etc?															
2. Purposeful communication . . . open-mindedness?															
3. Child-centred investigations?															
4. Skills . . . observing . . . predicting?															
5. Children devising tests?															
6. Children repeating tests . . . check results?															
7. Children extending work . . . applying learning?															

(5 schools represented. Most classrooms like this – 3pts, Some classrooms like this – 2 pts Few classrooms like this – 1 pt, No schools registered as zero)

my school-based support. For example, I ran centre-based sessions in which the teachers were given a simple investigation such as observing the changes in a lighted candle and then asked to communicate their findings in words, or art or music. Apart from reinforcing the links between cross-curricular areas, the teachers had to identify what was, for them, the essence of the changes as the flame flickered or the candle wax melted. The act of having to select, articulate and communicate the concept of say 'melting' increased their understanding of the processes of conceptual learning. In their classrooms the simple question, in an atmosphere where trust was established, 'What is it you would like the children to learn from this activity?' was enough to provoke thought and generate further ideas.

My results echo other studies that reveal the lack of repeat testing to check surprising outcomes of an investigation. Whilst we need to encourage more scientific behaviour, I now believe that the fact that children do not repeat tests may be partly due to the sense of 'hurry' that exists in many classrooms – so little time and such a lot to do – and 'It's tv time' or 'Assembly' or 'Playtime' again. Teachers and children are pressurised to cut corners and that can mean making fast deductions based on limited evidence. Can we do much to help here?

Teacher evaluation

1. Are there a variety of stimuli and resources being used effectively as starting points?
2. Is there acceptance that some mess, movement and noise is inevitable? Is there practical activity?
3. Does the teacher use questions which draw out connections and lead to further investigations? Does the organisation depend on context?
4. Is there a connection with everyday experiences in other areas?
5. Does the teacher use open-ended questions?
6. Is there sensitive and sensible encouragement towards valid conclusions through the above?
7. Does the teacher make records which indicate an awareness of the stage the child is at and an appropriate content balance?
8. Does the teacher use self-reflective techniques in discussions?

Teachers

In looking at the teachers' presentation in science, the data revealed that most teachers with whom I work provide stimulating environments for science to flourish. The changing behaviour in questionning technique was mentioned earlier and I actively encouraged this in courses and school support. The most significant feature is the lack of records kept in schools about the children's performance in science and the content they had studied. A great deal of support was necessary to help the teachers devise their own records, adapt mine or use commercially produced record sheets. Record-keeping is the area which has been the most difficult to promote. Although the weight of evidence and research argues strongly for it, opinion is still divided amongst teachers and advisory teachers. My own feeling is that when enough teachers have tried keeping science records, we will be in a stronger position to discuss the value of it, the criteria and methods of recording and using the information than we are now. Given the approaching recommendations of the National Curriculum document, it is even more important that teachers are familiar with science records and pupil evaluation for diagnostic purposes and progression.

Checklist 2. Teacher evaluation

	1	2	3	4	5	6	7	8	9	10	11	12	13	14	15
1. Stimuli . . . resources . . . used effectively?															
2. Practical activity?															
3. Further investigations . . . organisation?															
4. Connections . . . other experiences?															
5. Use of open-ended questions?															
6. Encouragement . . . valid conclusions?															
7. Records . . . appropriate content balance?															
8. Teacher . . . self-reflective?															

(5 schools represented. Most staff working this way – 3 pts Some staff working this way – 2 pts Few staff working this way – 1 pt No schools registered as zero)

The results showed me that although self-reflection is not well-developed yet, it is increasing. What I observed is that teachers are much readier to give themselves negative criticism than to mention their own successes and good teaching practice.

I am aware of the subjectivity in this kind of monitoring and generalisations and the small sample of teachers and schools observed, but the results have been significant and of great use to me and have helped me to evaluate my work as a Primary Science Support teacher.

School evaluation

1. Does the Head have a positive attitude and a commitment towards science?
2. Does the school have suitable resources which are accessible and used?
3. Are staff meetings held about the nature of science teaching?
4. Do the teachers' forecasts/records include science?
5. Does the school have a curriculum leader for science?
6. Is there much take-up of In-service courses for science (other than ESG)?
7. Is the school working towards a policy for science and a statement of it?
8. Is there a positive attitude and commitment to the ESG initiative?
9. Are there any significant factors that may affect the school/initiative? (eg. Other support teams in the school, etc . . .)

School

I was invited into the schools where I work by the headteacher and staff annd this meant that there was a positive attitude in the school from the start. The three biggest changes I recorded concern the occurrence of staff meetings on the science curriculum, the inclusion of science in the forecasts and the preparation of school science policy documents.

What have I learnt about supporting curriculum change?

It seems that for positive change to occur with the prospect of long-term implementation there must be certain conditions at the start:

1. The headteacher must give *active* support to the project.
2. There must be a curriculum leader for science with at least *two* other supportive colleagues.
3. The whole staff must feel involved and able to contribute to the project.
4. The project must be a long-term commitment (minimum 1 year).

Along with substantial school-based support it appears necessary for all the teachers to have some time out of the classroom (during school hours) for discussions and/or courses with colleagues from their own and other schools to increase their knowledge and understanding of science and improve their skills as educators in science teaching.

As an advisory teacher supporting change I have needed the following qualities and abilities (to start with):

– Ability to create an atmosphere of trust.
– Credibility as an ordinary class teacher.
– Adaptability and flexibility.
– Sensibility and discretion.
– Encouragement and a sense of humour.
– Being sure and clear about my own aims –

Checklist 3. School evaluation

	1	2	3	4	5	6	7	8	9	10	11	12	13	14	15
1. Head . . . positive . . . commitment?															
2. Suitable, accessible resources?															
3. Staff meetings?															
4. Forecasts/records . . . include Science?															
5. Curriculum leader for Science?															
6. Teachers – In-service in Science?															
7. Policy development . . . document?															
8. Positive towards ESG?															
9. Other factors (add comments also)															

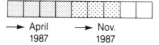

→ April 1987   → Nov. 1987

(5 schools represented. Very positive, or occurring regularly – 3 pts Satisfactory or occurring occasionally – 2 pts Not developed, or occurring infrequently – 1 pt No schools registered as zero)

setting achievable objectives – having realistic expectations.
– Ability to supply ideas and information.

Advantages of school-based support

Advantages of school-based support include:

a) Working alongside teachers on their 'home ground'.
b) Adapting to the individual teacher's level of experience, expertise and needs.
c) Relating the science teaching directly to the teacher's own class of children.
d) Relating the response directly to the conditions pertaining in the school.
e) Being a positive influence for science in the staffroom (an ambassador).
f) Being an opportunist and incorporating other cross-curricular activities into the science programme.
g) Being a guide through the difficulties, if any, of policy development and documentation.

Primary Science Advisory teachers could be viewed as curriculum catalysts and if they are effective, they make themselves redundant. School-based support does seem to be an important factor in effecting curriculum change. Reflecting on 2½ years of ESG support I am convinced of the benefits and my optimism for the future of primary science and technology is stronger than ever.

Bibliography

1. Blenkin, G.M. and Kelly, A.V. (1981) *The Primary Curriculum*, Harper and Row.
2. Harlen, W. (1988) *Teaching and Learning Primary Science*, Harper Education Series.
3. Whittaker, M. (1983) in C. Richards and D. Holford (eds) *The Teaching of Primary Science: Policy and Practice*. The Falmer Press.

* Max de Bóo is currently Lecturer in Education, Primary Science at Essex Institute of Higher Education.

MAKING AND DOING, NOT MAKING DO:
a review of Newcastle on Tyne's *Primary Technology Resource Pack*

Jim Campbell

Introduction

In June 1989, I visited the launch of the *Primary Technology Resource Pack* in Newcastle. The launch occurred, not in the best suite in the City Hall, but in a primary school on the Byker estate, where we could see the kind of work that the Primary Technology Resource Pack was intended to lead to. As you might expect the school classes were busy on activities involving designing and making, and the pupils were able to talk sensibly and articulately about how they had started off by discussing plans and ideas, how they had drawn sketches of the ideas and how they had used tools and materials to make the sketches a reality. They were also able to answer, with what I thought I detected as a long-suffering patience, the questions that journalists and educationalists put to them about how they might improve their models and designs. All very impressive, as is often the case when a local authority and school puts the work of its children and teachers and support services up for public appraisal.

Interested as I was in the work of the children, I was even more interested in how the teacher had developed it. If she was a technology whizz-kid, with a background in science, who had been working this way for years, then, impressive though the quality of the children's work was, it would not really be transferable to the classroom situation of normal teachers.

But she was not like that. She had no formal background in science or technology, and until a little over a year previously she had not done anything that she would now recognise as Design and Technology. But a year ago the school had become involved with the local authority's development initiative in primary technology, and she had been asked by her head to take responsibility for implementing technology in the school, supported by the work of the advisory service in Newcastle, including its ESG funded project on technology. One objective of this project was to develop a resource pack for teachers by working with them, and it was as a result of her response to the work of the project, that this teacher had been enabled to develop technology work with her children. Nor was she unique. According to the frontispiece of the pack, 'every primary school in Newcastle has a technology co-ordinator, and every school has been issued with the Primary Technology Resource Pack, in order to help the co-ordinators help their colleagues develop technology.'

The pack comprises some seven sections, about 110 pages altogether, and a videotape, presented in a durable ringbinder format, now so fashionable in curriculum development. My commentary below attempts to describe each section and analyse its usefulness for teachers looking for support, ideas and practical help.

The Primary Technology Resource Pack

Section One concerns **Technology and Primary Education;** it is a brief introduction to the principles upon which the pack is based. It makes the point that technology and design in primary schools should be defined in a simple way.

> 'Technology is a process that includes making something that works. ("Works" does not necessarily mean "move"; e.g. a chair works but does not move) ... design is the process of seeking a match between a set of requirements and a way of meeting them or finding an acceptable compromise.'

The emphasis on process in these two definitions is carried over into the approach that the pack encourages for schools:

> 'Science, design and technology are not so much to do with learning facts or isolated skills as to do with ways of thinking, investigating and making.
> Children should be encouraged to:
> a. form problems which are amenable to a practical solution
> b. observe and classify information
> c. suggest explanations in terms of cause and effect
> d. design and carry out practical investigations
> e. use knowledge and skills to solve practical problems
> f. design and make things that work
> g. communicate observations and ideas.'

This first section also briefly discusses Materials and Techniques, Evaluation, the Teacher's Role, and the cross-curricular contribution of Technology. The section concludes with five maxims, summarising its basic position:

> 'Technology is best in a topic
> Keep it simple

> Take up children's ideas
> First hand experience is essential
> Explore the cross-curricular work which is stimulated.'

Section Two is called **Getting Going.** It gets going, not by talking about technology in some abstract way, but by providing profiles of three teachers (two women, one man) 'new to technology', and showing how they had started, by having them write, in their own words, about how they first tried out technology, with photos of work in their classrooms. They do not provide rosy idealised pictures of how easy it all was for them, and their accounts are refreshing, realistic and encouraging. Thus one writes: 'I've made lots of mistakes. The most important lesson I have learned so far is to try and start in a simple way — keeping the design and materials as uncomplicated as possible.' Or another: 'I found the initial planning of technology quite difficult... (It) needs to be well planned; the greater the freedom the children are allowed, the more planning and organisation are needed from the teacher. The rewards, however, outweigh any extra work involved. Once children are familiar and confident with a technological approach they can, to a certain extent, organise their own activities.'

Next in this section there is some simple advice on planning for technology, together with two examples of Topic plans on Shopping, and The Fairground, and suggestions about how to plan and record children's work in these topics. There follow illustrations of how the design and technology aspects of these two topics have been developed in practice, together with related work in mathematics and language. Finally the section provides a lot of helpful and detailed advice about three aspects, viz., working with boxes, wheels and wood; pneumatics and hydraulics; and kits such as Lego, Lego Technic I and II, Quadro, Construx, Sticklebricks and others. This includes advice on essential classroom resources and equipment, ideas for simple box models, how to make axles and fixed and moving wheels, and powering simple models with elastic bands and motors. There is advice too on working in wood, after children have had some experience with less resistant materials such as paper and card. The comments on the kits are particularly helpful for those starting out in technology, since they give price, illustrate the kinds of activities that might be set, identify follow-up activities, cross-curricular links, and suggest scientific and other investigations that can be carried out using the kits.

By the end of these two sections, any teacher who wanted to develop her curriculum in Design and Technology would have a clear idea about the purposes of the subject, and some practical tips on how to get it up and running in her classroom. She would be able to adopt one of the topics, or apply the planning ideas to another topic, and if she had spent a couple of hours trying out the simple techniques illustrated in the last parts of the second section, she would have developed enough confidence and competence to feel that she could help the children where necessary. It is particularly valuable that many of the examples relate to Key Stage 1.

The next two sections are for extending the work after it has been implemented initially. They are called **Keeping Going** and **Controlling Models.** Keeping Going deals with aspects of classroom management, and ways of involving all children, not just those who take to technology easily, and with problems of matching tasks to children's capacities. It provides a checklist for helping teachers decide on appropriateness of tasks, which is simple but helpful, and it examines how to develop investigations out of the problems and difficulties that children encounter when models don't work, break, tip over, fall apart on first being used, and so on. The message here, given in very concrete examples from the classroom, is that every problem encountered is another learning opportunity. The section on Controlling Models covers manual, electrical and computer control. It combines a clear and lucid style, (both written and diagrammatic), with severe warnings on safety points, and lists of simple but essential equipment.

The fifth section is a one page introduction to alternative technology, called **Technology and the Environment**. The sixth section is a set of notes relating to the video tape. At this stage I should say that I started my appraisal of this pack by viewing the videotape first of all, before I even flicked through any of the rest of the pack. I expected the usual pictures with voice-over sound track, telling me how to interpret what I was seeing. But this video has been created by a group interested in media education, and is intended to emphasise that we as viewers actively construct what we see, and are not to be treated as passive receptors. So there is no voice-over, telling you what to think. All that happens is that you see, without any commentary at all, a series of sequences of technology in context — that is, design technology at work in Newcastle. There are images of magnificent Victorian cast-iron bridges, of boats on the Tyne, of the Tyneside Metro, of fire engines, ambulances and refuse lorries, of shopping centres and children's playgrounds. If you do as I did, and watch it before looking at the rest of the pack, you are left with hundreds of exciting ideas about design technology — and the realisation that you have not got much of a clue about how to put them into practice. This imparts even more purpose and usefulness to the rest of the pack.

The section of notes on the video, as a matter of fact, links very closely with the images, and provides both suggestions for following up visits, and some 15 topic planning sheets associated with topics on the video.

These are one-page webs, illustrating work in a range of subjects, including, of course, design and technology. A virtue of the video and the notes is that although they are very context-specific to Newcastle — they also alert you to the possibilities for similar work in your own environment.

The final section is a list of **Appendices**. This is extremely useful, and illustrates the care, and painstaking work that the authority has put into the pack to make it helpful. There is a Tools and Materials list, with the addresses of suppliers. There is a recommended Technology Toolkit, that should be available in each classroom. This kit has been planned and compiled to the LEA specification by CSO, Staniforth Road, Sheffield, and cost £14.61 in December 1988. By this simple action, the LEA has saved teachers an enormous amount of time and effort, since they do not have to scour catalogues, talk to other teachers, or fret about where to get the best deal. They simply have to send off for the kit. Similarly there is specified, from the same suppliers, a Newcastle Electrical Pack. It is recommended each school should have one of these, at the very least. There is a list of fiction and non-fiction books related to topics, and some other appendices relating to other parts of the pack.

There are two weaknesses in the pack. First it does not adequately deal with assessment. There is material on record keeping in a general sense, but little that would help teachers develop the kind of assessments that the national curriculum is going to require. Secondly, although the pack acknowledges that children need to acquire 'respect for the ways in which people of different cultural backgrounds, past and present, have shown their ability to enrich their environment,' there is little to help teachers incorporate multicultural aspects of Design and Technology into their classroom practice. Against this, however, the pictures of children and teachers at work, unselfconsciously show girls and women active in Design and Technology. In itself this is a strong contribution to equal opportunities.

Conclusion

A resource pack on its own, however good it appears to be, will not lead to real curriculum development. For a resource pack to be effective in helping teachers bring about change there have to be three other conditions, in my view. First, there has to be a framework of proactive policy-making and continuing support from the local authority, including funding. This kind of policy making gives the pack an identifiable set of values to which teachers can relate. Furthermore, through the identification and provision of a support service of advisory teachers, it enables teachers to call in help and guidance where necessary. The pack alone may be insufficient in the early stages of a school's development. Secondly, the pack must not have been created *for* teachers, but *with* them, embodying their practice and experience. This makes the suggestions in the pack easily incorporated into the practice of schools. Thirdly, it has to be very practical, recognising the different starting points of teachers, and children, in relation to development of technological skills. It must unashamedly provide tips, and sources of materials and equipment, for those who have never done any technology; and at the same time contribute to the further development of those already possessing some confidence. On all three criteria, the Newcastle Primary Technology Resource Pack is to be judged successful. If your local authority has a support system, but no resource pack; or provides guidelines, but little support, you could do a lot worse than buy this pack as the first step to implementing Design and Technology in your school. It will help you do most of what the national curriculum requires of you in Design and Technology, whilst enabling you to retain active learning, based on first-hand experience, and to use children's ideas as well as your own.

Note

The pack costs approximately £45.00 and is available from The Primary Technology Project, Pendower Hall, West Road, Newcastle NE15 6PP.

ASSESSING DESIGN AND TECHNOLOGY: some possibilities and problems

Moyra Bentley and **Jim Campbell**

Assessment of children's performance in Design and Technology, like assessment of other aspects of the national curriculum, has to be informed by the proposals in the Report of the Task Group on Assessment and Testing.[1] Two important principles were identified at the beginning of the report. These are:

that teaching, learning and assessment are, or should be, interrelated; and,

that the curriculum should lead assessment, not vice versa.

'Promoting children's learning is a principal aim of schools. Assessment lies at the heart of this process. It can provide a framework in which educational objectives may be set, and pupils' progress charted and expressed. It can yield a basis for planning the next educational steps in response to children's needs. By facilitating dialogue between teachers it can enhance professional skills and help the school as a whole to strengthen learning across the curriculum and throughout its age range.

The assessment process itself should not determine what is to be taught and learned. It should be the servant not the master of the curriculum. Yet it should not simply be a bolt-on addition at the end. Rather it should be an integral part of the educational process, continually providing both "feed back and feed forward". It therefore needs to be incorporated systematically into teaching strategies and practices at all levels. Since the results of assessment can serve a number of different purposes, these purposes have to be kept in mind when the arrangements, for assessment are designed.' (paras. 3/4)

The final report of the Design and Technology Working Group[2] gave some attention to the relationship of teaching, learning and assessment (in Chapter 4), and was explicitly influenced by the TGAT report. It stressed the point that appropriate assessment in Design and Technology could not be carried out by simple tests of a bolt-on kind. It would need to be holistic in character, and part of normal classroom activities — features that many primary school teachers will find user-friendly. The working group accepted that there was

'a powerful argument for assessment of design and technological capability to be based on the whole task which pupils carry out in their design and technology lessons. Anything less than this, for example a test of pupils' understanding of a body of knowledge or their ability to exercise a skill, independent of the context of specific design and technology tasks in which pupils are engaged, would lose validity.' (para. 4.8)

Much attention has been focused on SATs, partly because of the apparent importance given to them by various documents from the NCC, SEAC, and the DES, including the report of the

Design and Technology Working Group. SATs are the Standard Assessment Tasks carried out at around the age of seven and eleven for most children in a class. They are, however, only a small part of the assessment process, and concentration on SATs tends to play down two issues. First the ages of seven and eleven are reporting ages, not assessment ages. Assessment is to be carried out at all ages. And secondly, Teacher Assessment (that is, teachers' judgments of children's learning in classroom settings throughout each key stage) is much more significant than SATs for the assessment processes of the kind outlined above. Therefore it is to the issues associated with Teacher Assessment that this chapter is directed.

Assessing children's learning: an example

A class of top infants was carrying out a project on the theme 'Shopping'. As part of the work the teacher had suggested that in small groups they should make a till for the shop they had set up in the classroom. One group had done some planning of the design, with the help of the teacher. She had helped them raise some simple design questions. For example, what parts has it got? How big is it? How many partitions does it need for the different kinds of money? How can the drawer fit properly when it has a lot of money in it?

The second stage of the planning was 'imaging', when the pupils sketched designs and discussed the kind of materials they would need, e.g. large box for the till structure; small box for the drawer; card for partitions; coloured card for the totals display. This stage was also when the pupils talked through the problems together and attempted to agree how to proceed.

The next stage was the construction of the till, and testing how well it performed in the shop.

A final stage involved the appraisal of the till, including talking about how the 'shopkeepers' had found the till working, and writing a brief evaluation of the project, using the word processor.

A considerable amount of work in other subjects also arose in this project; mathematics for measuring size and proportions, for probability, concerning which coins are given out for change most frequently; English through co-operative discussion, and writing for a clear purpose. And there was further work in Design and Technology/Science by testing various kinds of shopping bags. However, we are concerned here with how a teacher might assess the work on the till for design and technological capability. There are three obvious ways, which lead to three

sources of evidence that a teacher can use for planning the next design task, and for recording against the statements of attainment.

First, when the teacher was discussing the early planning activities with the children she would have been able to observe their planning strategies, and if she had the appropriate list of levels of attainment statements, could quickly note, with a highlighter pen, which levels the children seemed to be working to. Second, the children themselves, in producing plans, sketches and diagrams, would be producing evidence that could be used to identify planning processes. Likewise the working model, and the pupils' written evaluations would enable the teacher to place the children's work on an appropriate level of the statements associated with the target 'Appraisal'. Over the longer term, the application of this experience to a new design problem, would allow for the assessment of a child's developing capability to be assessed and recorded.

Sources of evidence for assessment

Thus there are at least three connected sources of evidence that teachers can derive and use from topics concerned with Design and Technology. First there are *teacher observations* of small groups of children as they engage in the design process itself. Second, there are the *products* of children's work, which might include plans, comments on plans, sketches, written work, as well as the models made. This might be thought of rather as Art students' portfolios of work in progress are thought of in Art schools. It would include critical evaluations (appraisals) by the children themselves where appropriate. Thirdly, there would be *teachers' and pupils' notes* on the way the pupils applied previously learned knowledge and skills to new, related, problems. This would often involve improving existing designs.

Four unresolved issues

So far, we have presented a positive and relatively unproblematic picture of the processes of assessing Design and Technology, partly because we believe that what is being proposed has great merit educationally. But it would be naive to imply that there are no difficulties. We have identified four of particular concern to class teachers.

1. Resources

The most precious resource is teacher time, and in respect of assessment through observation of small groups or individuals, there is a resource

INDEX

implication. Some observations can be carried out without the presence of another professional in the room, but detailed and reliable observation of the processes of children's interactions in co-operative activities can only be carried out if the teacher doing the observing is not also managing the whole class. This need not be frequent, but it must happen sufficiently often for the teacher to have confidence that her observations are accurate. There is also the time needed to establish and maintain effective working record-keeping in this as in other subjects.

A further call on time will be made by the need to enable teachers within a school to experience Inset that helps them share and refine their judgments of pupils' learning. This can be thought of as an in-house moderation exercise. As the TGAT report argued (paras. 224/225) without this kind of resourced support it will be difficult to secure teachers' commitment to the activity itself.

2. Curriculum overlap

There is considerable concern that teachers will be overburdened by the demands for assessment — a sense amongst teachers that they are going to be continually, and continuously engaged in assessment across each curriculum area. It is quite clear that some topics in Science can contribute to assessments in Design and Technology, and equally it is clear from the Final Report of the Design and Technology Working Group that some topics in that area could provide the basis for assessments in mathematics, science, English, and other foundation subjects. But teachers will need to build up a systematic selection of topics on a whole school basis, that will help them assess in an economic and efficient manner. At the present time that task has hardly begun mainly because of the pace of current innovation. One possible answer is to plan topics that are mainly in one area, but which feed into a few others, rather than plan a topic, on say Flight, and think of ways of levering *every* subject into the topic web. Just because the topic is on Flight, there is no need to do Angels, in order to cover RE.

3. Baselines

Children come to the starting line of the national curriculum with different handicaps and advantages. A major issue concerns the baseline from which children, especially those in the early childhood years, can be assessed fairly. TGAT argued against adjusting results from assessment to take account of social factors, and this is perhaps understandable in a system whose main purpose is formative. However, as children enter Key Stage One, they will do so with very great variation in the experiences relating to Design and Technology. Some will have had rich experiences in pre-school settings such as those reported by Matusiak in this volume. Others will have had very little in the way of systematic education in this field. The implication for class teachers here is that they will have to find ways of identifying the skills and abilities that all children bring with them to school, through diagnostic assessment in classrooms. This also assumes the existence of a support system available to teachers for this purpose, but as yet such support is not universally provided.

4. Design and Technology co-ordinators

In the initial stages of a school's development of Design and Technology, and perhaps most crucially in the area of assessment, the delegation of responsibility for the subject to an identified co-ordinator would be of great help. Such a person could help teachers develop confidence in the subject and in the assessment procedures very quickly; perhaps, if the teacher responsible is confident and competent in the area, within a year. However, there is a massive shortfall in the numbers of teachers with expertise in this area, and without intensive and well resourced support from advisory teachers and others, it will be difficult for school staff as a whole to build up the confidence in their ability to assess children's performance fairly.

Thus the potential for an exciting and progressive pedagogy and assessment is clearly signalled — most clearly, perhaps in the commitment to holistic approaches outlined in the final report of the Design and Technology Working Group. But this potential will be rendered down into cynical and unproductive weariness, if teachers see themselves as expected to implement a high quality assessment system, without the resources — time, training, and equipment — for which it calls.

References

[1] DES (1988) *National Curriculum, First Report of the Task Group on Assessment and Testing.* HMSO.
[2] DES (1989) *National Curriculum, Design and Technology for ages 5 to 16.* HMSO.